THE

FOURTH BATTALION
THE KING'S OWN

(Royal Lancaster Regiment)

AND

THE GREAT WAR

Lieut.-Colonel W. F. A. WADHAM

and

Captain J. CROSSLEY

CONTENTS.

FOREWORD

*T*HESE *notes have been compiled, more or less in the form of a diary, with a view to placing on record the services of those who voluntarily came forward to serve their country in its hour of need.*

WALTER F. A. WADHAM.

February, 1920.

THE FOURTH BATTALION THE KING'S OWN REGIMENT AND THE GREAT WAR

Notes by Lieut.-Col. W. F. A. Wadham, V.D.

CHAPTER I.

Early Days.

THE year 1914 will for ever be looked back upon as the most memorable in the history of the Battalion.

The outbreak of the Great War in the month of August of that year caused the Mobilization Scheme, over which for years past each succeeding Adjutant had, in his turn, burned much midnight oil in endeavours to bring up-to-date the efforts of his predecessor, to be put to the test.

On Sunday, August 2nd, of that year, the Battalion proceeded to Camp at Kirkby Lonsdale to undergo the usual fourteen days' Annual Training as one of the units forming the West Lancashire Brigade of the Territorial Force. War and rumours of War then filled the air, and, upon arrival at Kirkby Lonsdale, a warning was issued by the Brigade Commander (Colonel G. L. Hibbert, D.S.O.) for the units composing the Brigade not to make themselves too comfortable, nor to make preparations for any lengthened stay, as orders had been received to detain the trains in which the troops had arrived, and further orders for the troops to return to their peace stations were hourly expected. These orders duly arrived in the early hours of Monday, August 3rd, and at 9-30 a.m. the Battalion started on its homeward journey, after the shortest Annual Training on record.

The Detachments proceeded to their various peace Headquarters, and the men were dismissed to their homes, with a warning that, in the event of the expected Mobilization taking place, they would be immediately recalled.

Germany having violated the neutrality of Belgium by attempting to utilize that country as a high road to Paris, Great Britain declared war on Germany on the 4th August, 1914, and on the night of the 4th/5th, orders were issued throughout the country for the Mobilization of the Territorial Force. The Mobilization telegram reached Headquarters about 6 p.m. on the 4th, and notices were at once issued, and the Battalion began to assemble at 5 a.m. on the 5th, for Medical Inspection. At 7 a.m. the Headquarter Companies had been medically inspected and at once left to guard the Kent and Leven Viaducts and by 4-30 p.m. that day, with the exception of the guards left by the Ulverston Detachment to protect the Kent and Leven Viaducts and by the Millom Detachment to protect the Duddon Viaduct, the Battalion had assembled in Barrow, and, under the command of the Officer Commanding Barrow Coast Defences, taken over important duties in connection with the protection of the works of Messrs. Vickers and the Harbour and Docks of the Furness Railway Company. Headquarters were established in the Holker Street Schools, and the surplus men, not required for guards, were billeted there.

Little of any importance or worthy of note occurred during the time the Battalion was stationed in Barrow, an air-raid scare, involving the standing to arms of all ranks for several hours in the middle of a very cold night, forming the only excitement.

The time was chiefly devoted to obtaining mobilization stores, ammunition and equipment (not forgetting transport, which, in these early stages of the war, was a most heterogeneous selection, varying from a milk float to a motor lorry, with water carts commandeered from the Local Authorities). The animals necessary for their haulage were an equally varied selection, including about every kind of " hairy " from a polo pony to a Clydesdale.

It was generally expected that the Battalion's next move would be to Ireland, and the advance party started off for that destination on the morning of August 8th, only to be recalled from Liverpool later in the day, owing to an order having been received cancelling the move.

On the 10th the Battalion was relieved from all duties in connection with the Barrow Defences, these being taken over by another Battalion, and on the 11th orders were received to move to Ulverston that day. The Battalion left Barrow at 6-15 p.m. on the 11th, and proceeded by road to Ulverston, arriving about 9-15 p.m.

In Ulverston the men were billeted in the Victoria Grammar School and the Dale Street Schools, Headquarters being established in the former. Whilst stationed at Ulverston the fitting out with equipment and drawing of mobilization stores was continued, drill and route marching filling up the time. On the 15th August orders were received (at 2-45 a.m.) to move to Slough for the purpose of guarding the Main Line of the Great Western Railway, between Paddington and Maidenhead.

The Battalion left Ulverston on the 15th, in two trains (the first at 10-30 a.m. and the second at 12 noon), and arrived at Slough at 7-30 and 10-30 p.m. respectively. The second train was delayed owing to one of the horse boxes falling to pieces at Crewe, thereby causing serious injuries to the animals it contained, and our first casualty, one of the horses being so seriously damaged that it had to be shot.

On arrival at Slough the Battalion was billeted in various schools for the night, and the following morning divided up by Companies. These were distributed amongst the different stations on the length of line—from Paddington to Twyford—allotted to the Battalion. Headquarters were established at Slough, in a large empty house with spacious grounds surrounding it, which quickly acquired the soubriquet of " Black Lead Castle," owing to one of its former occupants having rejoiced in the name of Nixey. A black cat, " which went with the place," succeeded to the title of the former occupant.

At the stations along the line the officers and men were accommodated in the waiting rooms, without bedding, furniture, or comforts of any description, and lived in these comfortless places for rather more than three months, during which period the Battalion was carrying out the duties of patrolling the line and guarding the bridges, etc., their food being sent through from Slough in dixies.

Great ingenuity was displayed by the members of the various detachments on the line in their endeavours to make their quarters, if not comfortable, at least habitable. The palm must be awarded to the Millom Detachment at Langley Park, where, under the able direction of the Company Cook, and with the assistance of a refuse tip alongside the railway, on which every conceivable kind of kitchen utensil seemed to have found its last resting place, a quite substantial and up-to-date kitchen was erected, and, with the aid of a huge Beecham's Pills (or other) advertisement board and some borrowed (?) waggon sheets, a commodious lean-to shelter was constructed. The homeliness of the shelter was completed by the addition of a tame fox, with which, contrary to the usual laws of animal affection, an Airedale terrier used frequently to indulge in gambols like those of a pair of kittens.

It was not to be expected that men fresh from the country, many of whom had never seen an express train before, could carry out these duties on a section of line such as the one for which the Battalion was responsible, without some casualties occurring. During the time the Battalion was employed on this duty several good men lost their lives in the service of their country, who would no doubt have preferably made the same sacrifice, had the opportunity been given them, against a more vulnerable foe than an express train.

The Battalion Reserve (chiefly composed of recruits) remained at Slough, where it underwent the usual course of Infantry Training, including a certain amount of Musketry at Runnymede, a very different thing however, at the beginning of the War, from the course of training which developed as the War proceeded.

It would be difficult to exaggerate the strain upon discipline involved in stringing out a Battalion of young and inexperienced soldiers upon a 30 miles length of railway, in close proximity to London and other places of interest and pleasure, or the additional responsibility thus thrown upon the Officers and N.C.O.'s, especially when all were anxious to proceed overseas at the earliest possible moment, and realized that, after being withdrawn from the duties of guarding the railway, it would be necessary for them to undergo a period of Battalion and Brigade Training before being considered qualified to do so. Naturally, some little impatience was displayed, but the Battalion's reputation for good discipline was well maintained.

Any spare time was chiefly devoted to football and cross country running, with a view to getting the members of the Battalion as fit as possible. The Battalion teams, drawn from all the stations on the line, achieved considerable success in both these forms of sport.

For the mounted Officers, and those aspiring to become mounted, the proximity of Windsor Great Park proved a great attraction, and effected considerable improvement in their equitation. The Golf Clubs of Stoke Poges and Burnham Beeches were kind enough to make the officers of the Battalion honorary members, but no time was found in which to take advantage of this privilege.

For the men a Club was organized by the Vicar, who was throughout most kind in doing all in his power to make the visit of the Battalion to Slough one which would call forth pleasant memories in the future. In fact, the general hospitality and kindness extended to all ranks of the Battalion during the time it was stationed in Slough was extraordinary, and was most gratefully appreciated.

Whilst at Slough an enquiry was received from the War Office as to whether the Battalion would proceed to Egypt to join the East Lancashire Brigade. To this a reply was sent to the effect that the Commanding Officer preferred that his Battalion should remain with the West Lancashire Brigade. At a later date an order was received to send two Companies to join the East Lancashire Brigade in Egypt, and these were withdrawn from the line and equipped ready to proceed. In the meantime a protest was made against the breaking up of the Battalion, and, at the last moment, after two Companies from a Battalion from the West of England had arrived at Slough ready to take over the duties of the Companies withdrawn from the line, a message was received cancelling the order, with instructions to return the two Companies to the West of England.

On November 9th the Companies of the Battalion, except those at Paddington and a few posts at other places, were withdrawn from the line, and on November 26th orders were received to move to Sevenoaks to join the remainder of the Brigade, which had moved there on the 11th. The Battalion left Slough in two trains, the first at 11 a.m. and the second at 1-15 p.m., on the 27th November, reaching Sevenoaks the same evening.

At Sevenoaks the Battalion was billeted in the St. John's end of the town, in empty houses, which, like the railway waiting rooms, were totally devoid of beds or furniture of any kind. The absence of any large buildings or halls suitable for drill, recreation or social purposes, in the area allotted to the Battalion, was also noticeable, and hardly conducive to comfort or efficiency.

The time at Sevenoaks was devoted to Battalion training, various areas for this purpose being allotted in turn to the Battalions forming the Brigade, amongst these being Knole Park, The Wilderness, Chevening Park, etc.

Musketry parties from time to time proceeded to Sandwich, Sittingbourne and Shoreham. The Battalion was also called upon to furnish a guard for the T.N.T. Store, which had been established in the caves at Chislehurst, and a visit of inspection to this guard invariably disclosed something of fresh interest.

Christmas, 1914, found half the Battalion still at Sevenoaks, and half at Sandwich for musketry, and, though some disappointment was caused at first by the edict that no Christmas leave was to be granted, all pulled together to make the best of the circumstances, and, with the kind and generous assistance of friends at home and newly made friends, the day passed off most successfully.

On the 22nd February, 1915, the billets of the Battalion being required for the accommodation of a Battalion of the New Army which was passing through Sevenoaks, the Battalion moved to Margate, where, on its arrival, it was received officially by the Mayor and Corporation, and proceeded to billets in excellent and well furnished houses at the Westcliff end of the town. During the time the Battalion remained in Margate, every kindness was extended to its members, and the visit will always be looked back upon by those who were fortunate enough to share in it (the guard at Chislehurst and the Musketry Party at Shoreham missed it) as a pleasant interlude in the hardships of training for war ; the only regret connected therewith being the brevity of its duration.

On the 28th February the Battalion returned to Sevenoaks, only to receive orders on the 1st March to proceed to Tonbridge before 11 a.m. on the day following. During the period at Sevenoaks many warnings of a sudden move, including one to the East Coast for immediate service after the bombardment of Scarborough, which arrived just as the Battalion returned from a twenty miles march, reached the Battalion. Although none of these materialized, they naturally caused uneasiness at the time.

The Battalion left Sevenoaks at 10-30 a.m. on March 2nd, and proceeded by road to Tonbridge, arriving about 1 p.m. At Tonbridge the Battalion occupied billets at the south end of the town, and was stationed here until April 18th, the time being devoted to Battalion training. As, however, it was called upon to furnish guards at Dungeness, Birling Gap and Cuckmere Haven, in addition to that already provided at Chislehurst, the strength was considerably diminished, and there was little opportunity for the Battalion to assemble as a complete unit. In spite of this, steady progress was made in the training, and frequent route marches with full equipment, combined with night operations at intervals, contributed towards the hardening of the men, who were rapidly getting into first-class fighting form. Games were not neglected, and, on Easter Monday, most successful Athletic Sports were held on the grounds of the Tonbridge School, very kindly placed at the disposal of the Battalion for the occasion.

On the 14th April warning was received that the Battalion was shortly to move to Bedford to join a Lancashire Brigade in the 51st (Highland) Division, and to proceed overseas with that Division at an early date. The Battalion left Tonbridge at 5-55 a.m. on April 18th, and arrived at Bedford at 9-20 a.m., its arrival creating a most favourable impression.

At Bedford the time was chiefly occupied in handing in old clothing and equipment, and receiving and fitting new. This exchange included new transport—both animals and vehicles—the mixed assortment which had so far served the purpose, together with a large assortment of antiquated and superfluous stores of every variety, having been left behind at Tonbridge.

The long period of training at home came to an end on the 3rd May, 1915, and in the afternoon of that day the Battalion left Bedford to join the British Expeditionary Force on the Western Front.

During this early period of the war, various problems as to how to obtain a sufficient number of men to send overseas and to retain an adequate number to carry on the work in munition factories, seemed to be perplexing the minds of the authorities, the uncertainty as to the right course to adopt having anything but a beneficial effect either on recruiting or training.

At first, returns were called for asking for the number of men willing to transfer from the Territorial Force to the Line Battalions, but this met with little response. Then returns as to how many men would volunteer for foreign service with the Line Battalions were called for, with similar results. Eventually, and happily, it was decided to ask the Territorial Battalions to volunteer for service overseas as complete units. This they did practically without exception. At first each man was given the opportunity of deciding for himself whether he would serve overseas or be transferred to a second line unit for service at home, but, later, only men unfit for general service were posted to the second line.

As regards the men required for munitions, the fact that the Battalion was drawn from an area in which the Barrow works of Messrs. Vickers were situated, caused great difficulty in obtaining the necessary number of men to recruit its ranks up to war strength. In addition to this, the constant withdrawal of men —chiefly those formerly employed by Messrs. Vickers— who had already undergone a lengthened period of training, and of whom several had become efficient N.C.O.'s, was a severe handicap. The result of these conditions was that the Battalion was not sufficiently up to strength to proceed overseas with the remainder of the Brigade, the units of which commenced to leave Sevenoaks during the second week in February, 1915.

This caused much chagrin and disappointment, which was, however, somewhat mitigated by the confidence in the efficiency of the Battalion manifested by the higher authorities in entrusting to us so many onerous and responsible duties and, eventually, sending it overseas when very considerably under strength, and at a time when the situation in the war area was extremely tense.

The route was via Folkestone and Boulogne, the transport having proceeded in advance via Southampton and Havre. The channel was crossed in the dark, darkness still prevailing on arrival at Boulogne, and deluges of rain added to the discomforts of disembarkation. The remaining hours of the night were spent in the camp on the top of the hill, a wind-swept place where the Indian tents, at that time, provided poor shelter.

After breakfast the following morning (May 4th), the Battalion started off down the other side of the hill to the station, and here joined the train conveying the transport from Havre, speculation as to its destination being somewhat rife. So far as the railway journey was concerned the destination proved to be Berguette, from which station the Battalion marched to Ham-en-Artois, and joined the Brigade.

Here the Battalion had its first experience of close billets in a foreign land, and those to whom a barn, with some hay or straw in it, was allotted, considered themselves literally, as well as metaphorically, in clover.

In these early days of the war everything was exceedingly primitive, not only with regard to the billets, but also the food and feeding arrangements. However, stout hearts and good spirits overcame all difficulties, and the time for which all had been waiting so long, viz., to get overseas, having at last arrived, the realization of this ambition caused all hardships and discomforts to be accepted cheerfully.

The Battalion remained at Ham until the evening of May 6th, when it moved via Busnes, Robecq, and St. Venant, to Calonne-sur-la-Lys, to form a reserve for the Fromelles show. A long distressing march was carried out by the Brigade in darkness and rain lasting throughout the night, during which progress was frequently delayed by other troops at cross roads, railway crossings, etc.

At Calonne the billets were very similar to those at Ham, the Headquarters being established in an old Mill House. Whilst here the Battalion thankfully made acquaintance with the baths improvised for the troops, and the opportunities offered for a change of clothing. The members also had their first introduction to Indian Native Troops, units of the Meerut Division coming in to rest and refit during the time the Battalion was at Calonne. The town was well within the sound of the guns at the front, and at night the sky was brilliantly illuminated by their flashes.

On 13th May the Battalion moved to Meteren (in readiness to proceed to Ypres), via Merville, Neuf Berguin and Vieux Berguin, taking over billets from the Canadian Royal Field Artillery. Whilst the Battalion was in Meteren the first Artillery of the New Army to arrive in France passed through, and the Horse Show provided thereby provoked the admiration of all beholders.

May 19th saw the Battalion move southwards once more, through Bailleul and the two Berguins, to La Gorgue, near Estaires—another long wet night march. Here it occupied the filthiest billets so far met with. Large numbers of both officers and men were allotted the buildings, including the Chapel, of a Convent School, the floors of which were inches deep in mud, whilst the grounds surrounding the buildings seemed to have been used for some time as the town refuse tip.

Luckily, another move further south to Locon, was made next day. This was a much more habitable and congenial spot, where the proximity of the La Bassee Canal afforded facilities for bathing, and the town of Bethune, in spite of daily shell fire from the Huns an excuse for a ride.

The only incident to be recorded during the stay of the Battalion in Locon was an ear splitting competition between a battery of French " 75's," which arrived in the village one evening, and a thunderstorm, which seemed to resent its presence. The thunderstorm won, and, incidentally, did considerable damage.

Whilst in Locon one N.C.O. and two men from the Lincolns, with experience of trench warfare, were attached, as instructors, to each Company, prior to their going into the trenches at Richebourg L'Avoue. In later days New Army Battalions were sent into the trenches in driblets—" opposite numbers "—Platoons and Companies, to mix with trench troops and become well acquainted with trench duties before taking over duty as units, but the Territorial Force had no such preliminary training. The Battalion subsequently had

B

the honour of initiating several Battalions of the New Army into their duties.

The night of the 24th/25th May, 1915, marked the Battalion's first introduction to the trenches. It was allotted a section near the Ferme-du-Bois, in the neighbourhood of Richebourg L'Avoue, which it took over in the dark hours of the night, and where it underwent its baptism of fire with singularly little protection, owing to the inadequate and dilapidated condition of the trenches. However, it survived the ordeal with considerable credit, and, luckily, few casualties, a congratulatory order being issued by the Brigade.

On taking over the trenches at Richebourg L'Avoue, the first duty was to open up communication with the front line, and turn the parapet of the recently captured fire trenches round the other way so as to face the enemy, also to remodel and establish second and third line trenches and construct communication trenches and dug-outs, the existing ones being simply rivers of mud and quite impassable. When taken over there were practically no dug-outs and the men not actually on duty had to rest lying in the mud in the trench bottom, not even on duck boards, these luxuries being few and far between.

The bodies of troops engaged in the last assault lay unburied, and the collection of identity discs, the burial of the dead, heavy labour at trench construction, and constant readiness to repel a counter attack, heat and overpowering smell in the day, and intense cold at night, and, withal, a shortage of water, were the first experiences.

During the time of its occupation of these particular trenches, the Battalion produced a marked improvement in their condition. The only grievances given vent to by the men were their inability to reply to the Huns' game of long bowls, the noise created by the continuous night firing of the Ghurkas' Maxim Guns on the left, which disturbed their rest, and the difficulty of locating snipers.

On the night of May 28th/29th the Battalion was withdrawn from the trenches to take up its " rest " quarters at the Redout, near Le Touret. However, owing to the too assiduous attentions of the Huns, who commenced to shell the place heavily immediately on the Battalion's arrival, inflicting a few casualties, a further withdrawal to the village of Le Touret was made the following morning, and on the 1st June, still further back to the village of Riez-du-Vinage. Here the Battalion remained until the night of the 5th/6th June, when it again proceeded to the trenches.

This time the section allotted was a portion of the old German trench in the much-fought-over Festubert area, and these, again, were of very indifferent construction, both as regards their protective value and the facilities afforded for comfort. The Battalion was here subjected to several daily bursts of shelling at more or less regular intervals, the casualties inflicted being mercifully altogether disproportionate to the amount of ammunition expended.

On June 9th the Battalion found itself once more at Le Touret for a spell of rest, and on the 10th was moved further back to Cornet Malo, just as the Huns were getting the range of Le Touret.

It was with much regret that on the 10th June I was compelled to leave the Battalion and proceed home on sick leave, the command thereof devolving upon Colonel (then Major) Thompson.

This did not, however, entirely sever my connection with the Battalion as, upon recovering my health, I assumed command of the 3rd/4th Battalion at Blackpool on 13th December, 1915. This Battalion proceeded to Oswestry on 19th April, 1916, and subsequently (having absorbed the 3rd/5th Battalion) became the 4th Reserve Battalion in which—during my period of command—approximately 250 officers and 4,500 other ranks were trained and despatched in drafts to units serving overseas ; the majority joining my old Battalion, the writing of the further history of which I am content to leave in the able hands of one who continued to serve with it.

WALTER F. A. WADHAM.

13th November, 1935.

FOREWORD TO PART II

The task of writing the following pages has fallen to me. Now that the duty has come my way, I have done my best, after a lapse of more than fifteen years, with the material available, and am aware of many omissions and imperfections. These have been kept as few as possible.

The record is written primarily for friends in the Battalion. No literary merit is claimed, and should the book fall into the hands of the general reader, his indulgence in this respect is solicited. It has been pleasant labour (bearing in mind our glorious dead), and up to May, 1917, when I left the Battalion, I am not dissatisfied with the result. From that time onwards is another matter. I was reluctant to attempt a story in which I was a non-participant, and used every means to get this part written by someone more qualified for the task. I was unsuccessful, and it became a question of the record remaining unwritten, or myself making the most of the position as it stood. Fortunately, powerful support was at hand in the person of Lieut.-Colonel R. Gardner, M.C., who served with the Battalion throughout, and, towards the end of the war, attained Command. This Officer has edited, and largely re-written, considerable sections relating to this later period. More would have been warmly welcomed (especially dealing with the remarkable stand of the Battalion at Givenchy), but he is a busy man, and scholastic duties intervened. My very real thanks are due to Colonel Gardner.

Major N. E. Barnes, T.D., Major W. G. Pearson and Captain P. W. Powell, M.C., have been helpful, and I have drawn gratefully on Captain R. B. Ross' charming book, " The Fifty-First in France." (Hodder & Stoughton). Acknowledgement is due to the courtesy and assistance given by the Committee of Imperial Defence, the War Office, and Lieut.-Colonel R. J. Brook, C.B.E., D.S.O., the Officer Commanding 4th Battalion The King's Own Royal Regiment.

JAMES CROSSLEY.

Ulverston,
  December, 1935.

1/4th BATTALION THE KING'S OWN (ROYAL LANCASTER REGIMENT) AND THE GREAT WAR

—

This narrative commences on the 10th June, 1915, the date on which Lieut.-Colonel Wadham's notes entitled " Early Days " ends.

—

CHAPTER II.

FESTUBERT.

WE left England under the impression that our military training was complete. There was one item, however, of which we had learnt little, and that was bombing. It was now impressed upon us that this weapon would play an important part in trench warfare. A Bomb School was therefore formed at a farmhouse between Lacouture and Richebourg St. Vaast. Qualified instructors were appointed, and a party under Lieut. G. F. Taylor was furnished from the Battalion. Material was scarce and equipment primitive, consisting at first of the home-made Battye. These were roughly made of cast iron. The bombers had to cut their own fuses, fix them into the detonators, attach the patent lighter, and wire the whole together—a laborious and lengthy task. The bomb when completed was unsuitable for transport, but could be easily thrown. There were other types being tried, percussion and time fuse. The percussion (Hale) soon lost favour, and we went through many varieties of time fuse, the light and heavy R.L., the Pitcher and the Hairbrush, until finally a selection was made of the Mills bomb, which stood the test well, being handy, portable and effective.

We now had the misfortune to lose the services of the Commanding Officer, Lieut.-Col. W. F. A. Wadham, who was ordered to the Field Ambulance, and eventually to England on medical grounds. He had done fine work for the Battalion, and it must have been largely due to his efforts that we were enabled to land in France at all. The strain had taken its toll. It was bad luck to lose him, but medical opinion admits of no argument.

The Command devolved upon Major R. Thompson (promoted acting Lieut.-Colonel) with Major N. E. Barnes as Second in Command.

Rumour, always busy, had for some days prevailed that the 154th Brigade to which we belonged was to be entrusted with an operation more ambitious than usual, and for once rumour was correct. A conference was held at Brigade Headquarters at Locon on the 13th June, and at 7 p.m. the following day the Battalion left billets at Le Cornet Malo, and moved by Companies along the familiar Route C, to take over trenches at Festubert. The transport also moved nearer to the line at Le Touret. By 10 p.m. the Battalion commenced to arrive in the old British trench, and were all in by 11-30. Contrary to arrangements this trench was already occupied by the 1/6th Scottish Rifles, and room was made in the reserve trench. The intended operation was an attack by the 7th Division, Canadian Division, and our own (the 51st) on the enemy position on the line Chapelle St. Roch-Rue d'Ouvert. After a 48 hours' continuous bombardment our mine at Duck's Bill was fired. At 6 p.m. on the 15th our attack commenced under heavy artillery fire from the enemy. It was led by the 1/4th Loyal North Lancs. on the right, and the 1/6th Scottish Rifles, with the 1/4th King's Own and 1/8th Liverpool (Irish) in support.

" A " Company (less party selected from two platoons under Command of Lieut. R. Gardner for Brigade Relay Posts and less other details) were ordered to occupy and hold Sap L. 8.

" B " Company moved to the old fire trench, and " C " Company moved forward to take their place in support. " D " Company moved into support trench, and it was reported that two lines of German trenches had been occupied by 6-20 p.m. " D " Company were in position at 6-50 when a number of wounded of the 6th Scottish Rifles passed through. At 7-20 all reports from the front were satisfactory. At 8 p.m. " B " and " C " Companies were ordered to push on in support of the Loyals and Scottish Rifles, who asked for reinforcements. " D " were ordered to the fire trench and arrived at 8-25 p.m.

The progress of " A " Company (less detachment) to Sap L. 8 was delayed by blocks ahead, and bridges broken by shell fire, but they reached their position and performed their allotted duty. " D " Company moved forward to support the Loyals, and threw back their right flank whilst trying to get into touch with the Grenadier Guards. At 9 p.m. the last platoon of " D " Company was sent from the reserve trench to rejoin their Company in front. The 8th Liverpools commenced to arrive and moved two Companies to the old fire trench, and one to support. Battalion Headquarters got into touch with the firing line through Lieut. Taylor, the Bombing Officer. Lieut. A. A. Wright, in charge of the Machine Gun Section, was ordered to reinforce the firing line. This move commenced, but could not be completed and the machine guns were buried as the result of enemy shell fire. All the Companies concerned exhibited great gallantry and performed their duties with devotion, and showed fine discipline and steadiness, and excellent fighting qualities. Between 10 and 11 p.m. a retirement was ordered. " D " Company still tried to establish contact with the Grenadier Guards on our right, but this was not effected until some two hours later.

An Officer of the Loyals reported at Battalion Headquarters about midnight, but could give no clear information of conditions in front. At 12-30 a.m. on the 16th, the German counter-attack was delivered, artillery support was impracticable, heavy casualties had occurred amongst the Officers of the attacking battalions, no supports came up on our right, and our right flank was therefore in peril. Enemy pressure increased, and retirement along the line was effected in good order.

At 1-45 a.m. an order was received to re-form the Battalion in the reserve trench, and a Battalion from the 152nd Brigade moved up in support, the 8th Liverpools taking over the old fire trench. On relief the Battalion assembled at Le Touret at 10 a.m. on the 16th.

Such is the bare outline of events on this memorable night. Let us examine them a little more closely and see what they reveal. It would be natural to assume that the result of the encounter was negative, seeing that the relative positions of the opposing forces now remained as before. It had been rumoured that this Action was to synchronise with an attack on a large scale by the French between Arras and La Bassée, but this idea was dispelled when it was found that the troops on our right did not co-operate.

The educational effect on the Battalion was profound, and the young soldier, who less than twelve months before had stepped out along Dalton Road, Barrow, or Market Street, Ulverston, etc., with the gay irresponsibility of Saturday night, and was now thrown into this cauldron of war, recognized its realities in a way he would never forget. He had seen death in battle at close quarters, and was to look at things in a different light thenceforward.

Of course there were the inevitable casualties, matters that went astray, and bad luck. Five minutes after the attack commenced, the telephone line to Brigade Headquarters broke down, and messages had to be transmitted by the relay posts previously referred to. This part of the work was very well carried out under Lieut. R. Gardner of " A " Company. Lieut. Hewitt of " A " Company, the Assistant Adjutant, a most able Officer, was killed and his loss was severely felt. Lieut. Bigland of " B " Company was killed in the fire trench before the advance commenced, and it was never clearly known how Lieut. Walker met his fate. Captain W. G. Pearson with " B " Company followed up the Loyals in attack, and the Company was well inside the German lines when he was hit by shrapnel and went down. Unfortunately he could not be found when the retirement took place. He was eventually picked up by the Germans and made prisoner. Almost as trying, after the retirement was ordered, was the finding and evacuation of wounded and stragglers. Sergeant Bell did good work, returning again and again to the front so long as any could be found. Lance-Corporal " Tommy " Dixon also was prominent in this connection. The notorious " L. 8," a sap following the line of a natural ditch twining away from our trenches to the German lines, and in " peace time " one of the plague spots from enemy fire, was occupied by " A " Company (less detachments) and was most valuable as a defence post, and also as a covered way for getting our wounded back into our lines.

The element of surprise in this attack was lacking. The enemy seemed to be well-informed of our intentions. He held his reply to our bombardment until almost the very moment of our attack and then opened a heavy artillery fire on our troops in their assembly positions, and caused many early casualties. In the fighting in the German trenches the enemy had the advantage of an adequate supply of bombs, whereas our supply became exhausted and the bombers were handicapped owing to forward ammunition dumps having been destroyed by the enemy's artillery. The deciding factor, however, appeared to be the withering cross fire which the enemy was able to bring to bear upon our troops when crossing no man's land.

To the onlooker the scene was one of terrible grandeur. The bombardment swelled to titanic proportions. Looking towards the line the eye was dazzled with the multitude of lights. Now it was the flash of exploding shells, now the slow glare of Very lights and rockets arching in the sky. Sometimes the thunder of the artillery softened into a muttering, when the tattoo of the machine guns became audible. The suspense of waiting was almost unbearable.

And so from this action the Battalion emerged, sadly depleted in strength by five Officers (three killed, one wounded and prisoner, one wounded)

147 other ranks (ten killed, 32 wounded and missing, 58 wounded, 37 missing and ten sick). Sergeant Bell received the Military Cross, which must be almost a unique award to one so junior. It was, however, a fitting recognition of one who even at this early period of his service, showed a natural flair for soldiering, which his subsequent distinguished career has confirmed.

A Special Order by Brigadier-General G. L. Hibbert, D.S.O., Commanding the 154th Infantry Brigade was issued as follows :—

" The Brigadier has received personal instructions " from Lieut.-General Sir H. Rawlinson, Commanding " IV Corps to convey to the Brigade his appreciation " of the gallantry shown by all ranks in the attacks " of the 15th and 16th instant under very trying " circumstances.

" The Brigadier wishes to add on his own behalf his " appreciation of the pluck and spirit evinced by all " and while he deplores the heavy losses incurred " congratulates the Brigade on the fine fighting " qualities displayed."

At 6 p.m. on the 16th the Battalion moved from Le Touret to billets at Pacaut, where it " rested " until the 22nd. The blessed word " rest " developed into one of the standing jokes of this period, and this time took the form of General's inspection, when he complimented the Battalion on its recent work. Working parties were provided for the trenches, and these found and brought back our buried machine guns. All requirements in arms and equipment were replaced and the Battalion had a two hours' route march. On the 22nd we moved back to Le Touret, where the same routine of working parties was carried on. On the 25th we marched to Estaires.

The folly of hearkening to idle report was never more triumphantly proved than now. It had been in the mouth of everybody that another week would see us at Armentières, or even further north. The rumour did not go bare and ungarnished. The most unlikely things were prophesied. Before the week was old the exact date of our leaving the Western front and embarking for India had been determined to the complete satisfaction of everyone, and no one dared to dispute a rumour which had emanated from the padre, and had received his benediction.

The Division did *not* go to Armentières, nor did it go much further north. It took over trenches in the sector of Laventie, and it was to the village of Laventie that the Battalion now went to billet. Laventie had been entered by the Germans in October, 1914, and vacated after the lapse of six days owing to the pressure of stronger forces, or in conformity with the general plan. Although separated from the front line by a distance of only three miles, it was still inhabited by many of the citizens, principally on the outskirts of the town. The centre of this place, from which radiated all the chief roads, was marked by the ruins of the church, a mere shell, and as sad a spectacle as could be witnessed in all this martyred region. True to their faith, many of the Catholics still clung to their dearest possessions and one cannot fail to remember the brave nuns of the Hospice, who refused to abandon their infirm charges to the fury of the oppressor. We found the place was still shelled almost daily.

On the 26th the Commanding Officer, Colonel Thompson, and others inspected the trenches. The trenches in the sector of Laventie partook of the nature of breastworks, and were in a much better state of repair than those at Festubert and Richebourg L'Avoué. It would seem that the fighting in this quarter had not attained the same infuriate heat as elsewhere. The temporary fever during the operations for the seizure of Aubers Ridge had subsided, but the enemy still held the commanding ground ; and our line, forming a wide but not a deep re-entrant, skirted the base of the ridge from Fauquissart to Neuve Chapelle. The defensive system on the whole, seemed to be too insecure and vulnerable. Its liability to rupture, if subjected to the intensity of a bombardment and the crushing weight of a massed attack, appeared obvious to everybody. There was but one main line of trenches running parallel to the Rue Tilleloy, but in rear a succession of isolated forts, adequately served, fenced off this fertile country from the onsets of the enemy. Four of these fortified redoubts were strung along the Tilleloy Road from Chapigny to Fauquissart, and a fifth was isolated slightly in rear.

It was a task, therefore, of the first importance to provide an adequate defensive trench system, and the Battalion began to prove itself active in the necessary labour. The Germans, on the other hand, from whom we were separated at an average interval of 150 yards, possessed all the natural favours of the ridge. They had at least a triple belt of defence, with the additional advantage of numerous communication trenches. Behind their front line were farms capable of being put into a very solid state of defence, such as Ferme Deleval, Trivelet, La Distillerie, Les Mottes Ferme, and the Moulin du Pietre. As their line receded, the trees grew more and more abundantly, wherein they were able to conceal large numbers of guns. They had also the inestimable advantage of full observation from the ridge. Surmounting this high ground lay the village of Aubers, fed by a light railway. This natural bulwark, in the hands of skilful troops, could resist the strongest frontal pressure that could be brought to bear upon it.

At 8-45 p.m. on the 27th, Companies commenced to move off to take over trenches from the 8th Liverpools, and by 10-45 the relief was complete. This was not bad going considering that no trench maps were available. Periscopes also were not on view at this period. It was comparatively quiet in the trenches but it was soon found that sniping by the enemy was the order of the day. This was a nuisance as considerable work remained to be done on parapets, dugouts and communication trenches. Good progress was made notwithstanding, and in a few days improvement was apparent.

At 10 p.m. on the 30th there was a short bombardment by our artillery, and it is to be noted how short and inadequate our bombardments were at this time.

Even at Festubert when a serious attack was contemplated, and after intensive gun fire, it was
remarkable how much enemy wire was left standing
in virgin serenity and uncut.   This was not due to any
lack of skill on the part of the gunners, but to lack of
shells, which were understood to be limited to three
shells per gun per day.   Things remained quiet but
persistent sniping continued.   On the 2nd July we had
a visit by the G.O.C. the 51st Division, also Officers of
the 5th Gordons, who had received orders to relieve us.
Suspicions were being formed that the enemy was
laying mines to our detriment, and not only that, but
actually placing field guns in his front line.   At 9 p.m.
on the 3rd the relief commenced, and working smoothly,
the Battalion were all out of the trenches by 11 p.m.
and marched into billets close to Laventie Station.
Snipers had accounted for Privates Tyson and Dodd,
killed, and Sergeants Pickin and Clampitt, wounded.

The usual routine of rest billets followed, numerous
working parties for the trenches being furnished, and
much sanitary work had to be undertaken to make the
billets habitable.   On the 5th the Brigade paraded for
inspection by General Sir James Wilcocks, Commander
of the Indian Corps, of which we formed part, and the
General was good enough to express his satisfaction
with what he saw.   The Battalion sighed happily when
it was all over.   These functions of the highly placed
have an uncanny knack of raising fears and tremors out
of all proportion to the occasion, and it is not without
humour to reflect that the majority would cheerfully
prefer a turn in the trenches to one of these devastating
ordeals.

Up to this time organized bathing facilities were
non-existent, and it was only in intermittent streams,
accidentally met, that we could indulge the craving
for a thorough soak.   This, too, could only be gratified
at the expense of much diffidence, as it had to be
carried out in the vicinity of the local population.
This deficiency was now being overcome, and in
certain centres baths were in existence, where the
troops could revel in real hot water and soap.   This

was not all. They could hand in their soiled and inhabited underwear, and receive in exchange another set, sweet and clean, a boon indeed. One of these bathing centres was at La Gorgue, of dismal memory, but now changed to an enchanting oasis. The brewery had been taken over for the purpose, and the vats provided ideal receptacles for soiled soldiers in mass formation. Pandemonium, made up of songs, shouts and laughter, during these grateful ablutions, conveyed to the authorities approval of the wisdom of their kindly ministrations. It was, then, to the baths at La Gorgue that the Battalion marched by Companies on the 7th and 8th, and returned refreshed and enthusiastic.

Working parties went out nightly to the trenches, where the task of strengthening the defences went on incessantly, one of the parties being shelled en route, and two men were wounded. The billets at Laventie too, received their customary shelling from the Hun, but the tortured church again bore the brunt, and no other damage was done, and there were no casualties. At 6 a.m. on the 9th orders were received to take over trenches, and in the evening the move commenced, the relief being completed by 10 p.m. The Battalion held the four posts and small ammunition depot in rear of the line, the trenches being held by the 4th Loyals and Scottish Rifles. On the 11th the Machine Gun Section went into the line in relief of one gun each of the Loyals and Scottish Rifles. The 12th was notable for the presentation to Sergeant Owen of the Distinguished Conduct Medal for the action at Rue d'Ouvert, and our snipers accounting for two of the enemy.

At 9 p.m. on the 15th the Battalion moved into the trenches in relief of the 4th Loyals and Scottish Rifles, and at 10-45 the relief was complete, but we suffered three casualties from rifle fire. On the 17th those insufferable pests, civilian snipers, were seen behind our line. A keen hunt for this new quarry was immediately organized, but without success for the moment. They are wary birds, and the nest is seldom near where they operate.

Evidence that further moves were in contemplation, not only for the Battalion but for the Division, was forthcoming when the trenches were visited by the Staff of the 8th Division, and the usual curiosity and conjecture was indulged as to our destination. It was interesting and intriguing, but, after past experience, fantastic forecast was absent, opinion more sober, and there was a disposition to " wait and see." This visit was speedily followed by orders for the relief to be carried out, and on the 23rd we handed over to the 2nd Royal Welsh Fusiliers. This was completed at 11 p.m., and at 11.30 the Battalion marched to billets at Estaires, near La Gorgue. Here equipment and clothing were issued, and on the 25th Lieut. E. Tillyard and one N.C.O. left by motor car for the new area on billeting duty. This area was now definitely understood to be the Somme.

CHAPTER III.

PICARDY.

Our stay at Estaires was short, and at 9.45 a.m. on the 27th we marched via St. Venant to Berguettes (where we had detrained on our first arrival three months previously), twelve miles distant, on the Nord Railway, and there entrained. The train consisted of the usual enormously long string of closed wagons " 8 Chevaux 40 Hommes," with here and there a dilapidated passenger coach. We passed westward through Hazebrouck and St. Omer, west into the night, and crept slowly over the flats, deeper and darker, until the twinkling lights of Calais, and the fresh fair faces of women, reminded us of home.

The first greys of morning were just showing through the trees when the sleepy-eyed Battalion, once freed from the choking confinement of the wagons, stretched its stiffening limbs and breathed a purer air. First impressions are as a rule deceptive, but our first impressions of the Somme, when we detrained that lovely morning at Mericourt-Ribemont, lingered for many a day as a sweet memory. The period that followed was one of inestimable preciousness to us. The free wholesomeness of the air, the fresh breezes that served but to stir the leaves and ruffle the pools, contrasted strangely with the clogging miasmas of Flanders. We felt ourselves excited with the discovery of a new world. The whole landscape to our appreciative eyes appeared to be lapped with a beauty as yet untarnished by the impurities of war. The skies were tricked out with a new colouring. In the north the dawn came up with splendours that were hidden from us. The mists blinded the sunrise in Flanders.

Lieut. Tillyard, who had motored south to arrange the billets, met us at the station with rosy accounts of our new area. His reception had been enthusiastic, if somewhat overshadowed by the superior attractions of the uniform of our Highland brethren of the Division,

especially the kilt, which was a source of unending
wonder to the local population.

We marched away from the leafy arches of Mericourt,
that seemed to invite the tired traveller to revel in
their coolness. New vistas opened out before us.
On our right hand a sugar refinery shot its well-known
ugly chimney into the skies. On our left hand a
roadside shrine seemed to invite a moment's medi-
tation. But there, in front, joy to our hearts, lay
the broad rolling uplands, topped with yellowing
corn, that went before the breeze in glistening waves.
There were a few early harvesters at work—old men
with sunken cheeks and women with toiling hands,
who paused for a moment to gaze at the novel sight
of the British " Tommee " on the march.

A new wonder now brought amazement to our faces
—those marvellous national highways that take no
account of contours, but run, arrow straight, for miles.
That on which we set foot at this time was known as
the " Route Nationale No. 29 de Rouen." From
Amiens to Albert it ran with scarcely a single deflection.
And, as was a feature common to all these national
roads, magnificent trees bordered it from end to end.
Even in the case of secondary roads attempts were
made to utilise the waste lands contiguous. Apple
and plum trees were growing by the roadside, their
boughs bending with fast ripening fruit. These were
all communally owned. France and Belgium are,
verily, the high schools of thrift.

The Battalion went into billets at the quaint and
attractive little village of Bouzincourt. It was not an
elegant village. Its houses all looked jerry built ; it
adopted no particular plan. Bouzincourt was the
communal centre of a large agricultural district.
There were no outlying isolated farms. All were
collected within the boundaries of the village, in order
to secure mutual protection. Each house in the village
had its barns and byres attached. One man was no
richer than his neighbour, and there was no incitement
to ambition. The men who remained, not subject to
the military levies, were all old men. About the

village the most distinguished person was the *curé*, whose air of aloofness and stern piety was spoiled by the fat and puffy appearance of his housekeeper, visibly addicted to snuff, so that all fine impressions vanished.

The Battalion was soon distributed round the village, the men in comfortable barns and the officers in the farm houses. Dinner had been prepared *en route* in the travelling kitchens, and was served immediately on settling down. Interest was languid and appetites mechanical, and, due to the incessant movement and cramped travelling of the past thirty-six hours, the troops sank into oblivion in this restful arcadia.

It is usually the unexpected that happens. Instead of going into the trenches straightaway day succeeded day in peaceful routine work, and this period of our history in France approximated more closely to a rest than any we had yet experienced. By this very immunity from trench cares we missed what must have been a most interesting experience—that of taking over trenches from the French army, who were now released for service elsewhere. This engaging duty fell to the 8th Liverpools, who took over the new sector on August 1st.

On August 3rd the commanding officer and two officers per company visited the trenches, which were to the east of Aveluy, a village three or four kilometres to the east of Bouzincourt, a direct road over a ridge connecting the two. This road, the top and eastern slope of which was in view of the enemy, was impracticable in daylight. A wide detour had therefore to be made via Engelbelmer and Albert. On approaching the latter place a first view was obtained of the damaged campanile of the church—the Eglise Notre Dame de Brebières—a pitiful sight and one to linger in the memory. The spectacle of the beautiful gilded statue of the Mother and Child hanging perilously head downward, through the vile attentions of the Hun, was moving in the extreme. There are some phases of this war to be dismissed with a smile, but wanton destruction such as this, the Cloth Hall at Ypres, Rheims Cathedral, and a hundred other tragic horrors of fallen stones, can evoke only tears. Nothing can atone for them, least of all German *Kultur*!

And so over the square, pitted with shell holes, out of the town again, three kilometres to the north, and under the light railway running to Guillemont and Combles, we come to Aveluy, a neat little village just behind the line. It has had its share of attention by the enemy, but is still inhabited by a section of the villagers. Down a declivity, at the bottom of which flow the waters of the Ancre—a considerable stream, limpid and pellucid, but suspect and taboo, as its head waters are in the German lines. Over the culvert and up the other side, past a roadside shrine, close to which are the ration and ammunition dumps, and, meeting more rising ground, we come to the entrance of the communication trench, which it was well to use.

The first effect of these remarkable trenches was speechless amazement. These were trenches such as we had never experienced hitherto. In the north we had been accustomed to sand-bagged breastworks; but here the trenches were deep and wound serpent-wise, in a fashion that left the stranger utterly bewildered. It was a labyrinthine system, constructed according to the suggestion of the natural contours, and not following any stereotyped plan, as at the Quinque Rue. On first acquaintance with these amazing passages it was impossible to move about with any assurance whatever. Not until a lengthy residence therein had made us familiar with the names could we walk about with a perfect sense of direction. The communication trenches crossed each other, doubled back, affected the most bizarre forms.

Our new trenches, designated " F.1" sub-sector, spread fanwise over a saddle of rising ground, disappearing on the northern extremity into Authuille Wood, which was of considerable size. The names of the trenches under their former French occupants had followed the system of perpetuating the memory of French heroes who had died for their country or otherwise rendered signal service. This system, admirable as it seems, was now being replaced by our own more practical method, and we found ourselves struggling from Post Donnet to Palatine, Fishergate, or John o'Gaunt Street. The Battalion frontage was extensive, approximating a mile in length. From its highest point, opposite Ovillers, a magnificent enfilading view disclosed the wreckage of La Boisselle, separated by a wicked little gut of very narrow width, known as Sausage Valley, from the divisional trenches further on our right, which were entrusted to our Highland comrades.

It was in these trenches that the French army had lived, relieved only at irregular intervals. In the parados men had dug holes, where, two by two, they slept like dogs in kennels, a curtain of rough sacking fixed by a rusty bayonet, serving as a protection from wind and rain and sun. Inside one eats, sleeps, sings, and sometimes dies. The shelters of the officers are a little larger, and the first-aid posts have the choice of security. Each company has its telephone and telegraph instruments. A liaison is established between all posts of command. Here men are reading, others are writing home those few words which mothers, wives and sweethearts alone cherish for their preciousness. There a stretcher-bearer is binding up a wound. By raising the head a strip of blue sky can be seen. Yes, the sky can be blue at the front, the flowers can bloom, and the birds can sing. Here and there was a piece of chalk carving in which the French " Tommies " were vastly skilled, or a welcoming banneret, such as " Pitou shakes hands with the British Tommy."

By their very scope and efficiency these trenches required constant vigilance and attention to keep them in repair, and the Battalion now began to furnish the usual nightly working parties for this purpose. Otherwise life in Bouzincourt continued its pleasant and uneventful routine. The weather was beautiful and the inhabitants kind and hospitable to the best of their limited means. One of the families stands out as a pleasing memory. M. and Madame —— were the owners of a roomy house standing back from the village street, the front laid out as a garden, full of old-fashioned and sweet-smelling flowers, geraniums, roses, hollyhocks and pinks. Monsieur was a *cultivateur* and looked after the outlying fields. The son was at the front, as was the husband of the eldest of two daughters, Germaine and Suzanne. The interior of this delightful household was as homely and attractive as the exterior promised, and the family kindness itself. The Battalion staff were allotted this peer of billets, and afterwards the transport officer and the writer had the felicity to succeed and so speak with authority and conviction.

On the 7th August, at 9 p.m., the Battalion marched over the ridge by companies to take over trenches from the 8th Liverpools, and so remained without a break for three weeks—eloquent testimony to their habitableness. From the first things were comparatively quiet, and we had to contend with only spasmodic shelling. On the 10th " C " and " D " Companies, on the left, were bombarded during the morning. The bombardment was intermittent, but " D " Company had an unpleasant time from 12 noon to 12.30 and had one casualty. On the 14th some little shelling occurred, and Private Burton, of " B " Company, was killed. A new duty, and one which caused some swelling of pride, was now imposed on us. For some time the new units of " Kitchener's Army " had been pouring into France, and very workmanlike they looked. Each night a company from the 6th Royal Berks, and later from the 8th Norfolks, arrived in our trenches for instruction and were relieved the following night by another company. A diversion of an even more pleasurable kind was to take possession of the Battalion from now onwards. We had been three months at the front, and thus qualified for the privilege of " seven days' leave." Parties were organised weekly and despatched on their way to England, to the good-natured envy of those left behind, who volunteered sound advice, which may, or may not, have been acted upon by the fortunate ones.

On the 16th our heavy artillery bombarded La Boisselle on the right, and the enemy replied later on our trenches. On the 17th there was shelling of our line, and Lance-Corporal Woodward, of " B " Company, was killed by a sniper, while on the 19th, after a very quiet morning, we exploded a mine at La Boisselle and put in some big shells later. The enemy retaliated with trench mortars and shrapnel and later his machine guns fired on the communication trench and the road to Aveluy, altogether rather a disturbed night. Private Robinson, of " C " Company, had his face grazed by a bullet. On the 21st the Battalion was relieved by the 8th Liverpool Irish and moved back to the support trench. The weather remained perfect, but the nights were cold. The companies held inspection of clothing and equipment and work was carried on with deepening two new communication trenches. On the 23rd five new officers joined the Battalion and were posted, Lieut. B. A. Leslie to " B," Second Lieut. H. H. Hodkinson to " A," Second-Lieut. C. G. Chapman to " B," Second-Lieut. G. J. Purnell to " C," and Second-Lieut. E. D. M. Meyler to " D " Company.

On the 28th August the Battalion was relieved by the Loyals and 5th Lancashire Fusiliers, and at midnight marched into billets at Martinsart. The weather had changed, and the move took place in very heavy rain, over muddy roads. This would have been bearable if decent billets had been available on arrival, but, with the exception of La Gorgue, these were the dirtiest and most dilapidated billets we had encountered. The surroundings of this depressing village were a sea of mud, where the unfortunate transport animals were picketed standing fetlock deep. The Battalion was in Divisional Reserve, and there were also located here details of the 1st Indian Cavalry Division Headquarters. On the 29th the Commanding Officer reported at Headquarters, 51st Division, at Senlis (a notable feature of which place were the natural underground caverns) and also at Headquarters, Indian Cavalry Division. Working parties were furnished on the 30th and 31st for work on the roads at Bouzincourt, and in the trenches. Bombing instruction was going on apace and three officers and one hundred other ranks attended the Bombing School at Aveluy. Officers from each Company also reconnoitred routes to Authuille, a small village north-east of Martinsart. Time was spent on much-needed repairs to billets, the weather continuing bad, more heavy rain falling at this time. A few small shells were put into the village but no harm was done, but on the 4th September ten more were dropped and Private Drinkall, " C " Company, was wounded.

On this evening billets were handed over to the 5th Lancashire Fusiliers, and the Battalion moved off to the trenches in relief of three Companies of the 8th Liverpools in the old line, relief being completed by 9.15 p.m. The night was very quiet. At 8 p.m. on the 5th " B " Company sent out a reconnoitring patrol in front of the barbed wire, who returned safely with some useful information. Soon after midnight on the 8th an enemy patrol was captured. This patrol of one Officer and three men came in at one of the listening posts on the left of the sector. They came down the front of our wire and were watched by our listening post, consisting of Lance-Corporal H. Martin and Private J. Carrick, " D " Company, who waited until they were quite close and then challenged. The enemy patrol at once surrendered. This capture was excellently managed. The following night about a dozen small calibre shells were sent over and the enemy appeared to be trying to locate our listening post where the capture had been made. On the 12th Lance-Corporal Martin proceeded to Army Headquarters, where he was presented with the Distinguished Conduct Medal and promoted Corporal for his recent fine work. We were now negotiating the maze of trenches with more confidence, and even the communication trenches held no terrors for us. In traversing this trench at night from the line one would encounter a weird apparition approaching from the opposite end, and more by way of greeting than challenge, would call out, " Who are you ? " and the reply, " O'll tell thi who I am lad, O'm a walking dump ! " was quickly confirmed when a shadow bearing a corrugated iron sheet, a roll of wire and a duck board brushed past to its destination in the front line. This gratifying intelligence genially imparted and duly assimilated, both went their ways ruminating on the queerness of things.

The trenches had been previously inspected by the 152nd Brigade, and on the 21st September we were relieved by the 5th Seaforth Highlanders. The Battalion moved into billets at Hénencourt, a rather longer march than we had had recently. We found the billets in fair order, but experienced some trouble with the Officers of an entrenching Battalion, which was eventually amicably settled. After this small *contretemps*, and after seeing to the needs of their men, some of the younger generation of our Officers started to forage for a meal for themselves and finally settled on the estaminet in the main street, " Au Petit Caporal," as promising the best results—a prescient choice. Any visitor to this village is strongly advised to call and ask for mutton cutlets. They will delight his heart. Let him also ask for Epernay, for the *cuvée* is above reproach. The hospitable Picard family of this inn included a grandam, on whom the asperities of advancing age had not yet begun to make an impression. She sat in her corner chair like a queen, very calm and dignified. Her regal manners and pleasing countenance, combined with a natural affability, were touching and striking proofs of a well-ordered household. Madame prepared our cutlets, while Mademoiselle, whose unaffected simplicity and distinguished mien proclaimed her at once a charming kitchen-lieutenant, was pleased to serve us.

The time was now spent in the usual " rest " fashion, holding inspections, making up deficiencies in kit, parades (not forgetting pay parades), and route marching. On the 26th the Battalion quitted billets and marched from Hénencourt to Aveluy. This march was not very well carried out and caused some concern to the Adjutant. It had been evident for some time that the step of the men was losing some of its wonted fire, and this could confidently be ascribed to long periods in the trenches, where, although there was an abundance of manual labour to be done, pedal exercise was out of the question. We took over the support trenches from the 6th Seaforths, the weather being wet and much colder.

On October 1st, Brigadier-General Hibbert, commanding the 154th Brigade, received a bullet wound in the shoulder when visiting Poste Les Dos, and we were sorry to lose his guidance. One man of " B " Company was also wounded at this post. An order was received reminiscent of earlier days after mobilization, when the Battalion was decimated by similar orders, for fourteen N.C.O.'s and men to return to England for work in the Hodbarrow mines, but our trench stores were enriched by the addition of forty-eight knobkerries—a fearsome weapon. We were relieved in the trenches by the 5th Lancashire Fusiliers and 4th Loyals and went into billets at Aveluy. Second-Lieuts. Ward and Keller joined and were posted to " A " and " B " Companies, respectively. Working parties for the trenches were provided, as usual, but the men preferred being in the trenches to proceeding there daily for work. On the 7th, Brigadier-General Edwards took over command of the Brigade, an appointment which, to our untutored minds, appeared unusual, he being a Cavalry Officer. On the 8th we were inspected by Major-General Harper, 51st Divisional Commander, taking over trenches and stores from the outgoing Battalion in the evening. On this occasion these were not found satisfactory. They strove to impress upon us that these trenches were a paragon of comfort to what they themselves had taken over. It was always curious to note how invariably sceptical of improvements were any new comers. The qualities attributed to the " last lot in " were never very flattering, but on this occasion we felt, with reason, that we had not received a square deal and rebelled accordingly.

A period of comparative quiet followed our taking over. Patrols under Second-Lieut. Hodkinson reconnoitred the ground in front of Ovillers, and Private Walker, " C " Company, was slightly wounded. The Battalion now encountered a further piece of bad luck on the 13th, when the Commanding Officer, Lieut.-Colonel R. Thompson, was sent to the Field Ambulance, wounded by shrapnel when in the fire trench, and the command devolved on Major N. E. Barnes. Problems for the new C.O. were soon forthcoming when Captain Jackson, the Adjutant, was appointed to act as Brigade Major. This officer had done well in knitting the Battalion together on and after mobilization, and, although we felt his loss severely, everyone was pleased that his qualities had been suitably recognised. He was a fine athlete, and many times had the Battalion in difficulties trying to emulate his tireless pace at exercise. Captain Tillyard was appointed to succeed him.

The usual spasmodic shelling, rifle and machine-gun fire was taking place in the trenches. On the 21st we were relieved by the 8th Liverpools, " A " and " D " Companies, and Battalion going to Lower Poste Donnet and "B" and "C" Headquarters to Poste Lesdos. The weather at this time was misty. On the 27th we were relieved by the Loyals and Lancashire Fusiliers, and went into billets in Aveluy. On the night of the 30th/31st the enemy fired about eighty howitzer and field gun shells into the village. The majority, fortunately, did not explode, and no billets were hit or damage done. Private J. Vincent, " C " Company, was killed, and Sergeant Wells, " D," and Corporal Holmes, " A " Company, wounded on a night working party. On the 2nd November we relieved the 8th Liverpools in the trenches. We found these in a very bad state. A large part of the fire trench in " C " and " D " Companies section had fallen in. Rivington and John o'Gaunt Streets were nearly impassable. Immediate work on these was imperative. This was again an opportunity for " D " Company to show its mettle. Many times had these men from Millom, iron ore miners in peace time, wrought wonders with pick and shovel, to the amazement (and admiration) of their less skilled comrades. The trenches at Aveluy were but one more achievement to their credit.

The weather was now definitely bad, cold, wet and the wind north-east. It will be convenient here to refer to the "comforts" which, since mobilization, had been collected and sent out to us by private enterprise. These comforts consisted of many things, principally wool underwear, socks and mufflers and tobacco and cigarettes. The Battalion was extremely fortunate in its friends at home, and the severe weather which now overtook us tended to emphasise those feelings of gratitude which were present at all times. On the 7th we were relieved by the 6th Argyle and Sutherland Highlanders, and proceeded by Companies to Hénencourt, where new billets were taken over, the next two days being devoted to cleaning rifles and the more difficult task of cleaning clothing. This was saturated with the thick, glutinous mud of the trenches, and it was almost impossible to make any impression on the greatcoats.

On the 10th, Lieut.-Colonel F. M. Carleton, D.S.O., assumed command of the Battalion. He was an ex-regular Officer of the Regiment, who some years previously had served as Adjutant of the Battalion. In addition to the D.S.O., he wore the ribbons for the South and West African campaigns and the Nile Expedition 1897. Almost at once the Battalion began to feel the influence of a new personality. This influence had the quality of the east wind, and, with all its tonic properties, the Battalion felt impelled to brace itself unwontedly to meet its cutting edge. Our education was not yet complete. We continued in rest billets at Hénencourt until the 16th, when we marched to Authuille to relieve the 7th Gordons in "G.1" subsector. The transport moved to Martinsart.

This new area, just north of our previous line at Aveluy, had previously been reconnoitred by our

Officers and was, therefore, more or less familiar. It was roughly the segment of a circle, of which the centre was the village of Authuille. The boundary radii were Campbell Avenue and Thiepval Avenue. The former followed the course of the road that inclined from Authuille to Ovillers. The other avenue led direct to Thiepval of evil fame, until the bulwark of our front line rudely cut it short at a point where a solitary telegraph pole shot up out of an immense wilderness of weeds. Within this circumscribed area were many once excellent trenches, but now in bad condition, and a few on which a malevolent influence seemed continually to rest. The shelters as they existed were designed to withstand only a moderate shelling, were in poor condition, but they fulfilled our modest expectations. All were accommodated in trenches or shelters, including Headquarters, except the latter's Mess. Some inspired scout had discovered a disused and comfortable cellar in the village, and this provided an excellent mess room. It was a very quiet period.

On the 22nd we were relieved by the 4th Loyals and went into dugouts in Authuille. The chief desideratum was to keep warm, and the demands on the Quartermaster for coal, coke and charcoal for the braziers were peremptory. In the conveyance of these supplies the writer witnessed a small epic in transport. The route led from Martinsart, where Driver " Dorcas " Dixon harnessed his pair of mules to a limber and departed, loaded above the military Plimsoll line. These mules, the pride of their driver, were sleek creatures, slender-limbed and thin-flanked, with a gliding motion deceptive to the uninitiated. Skimming along with their $2\frac{1}{2}$ ton burden all went well until, half-way through the Bois d'Aveluy, the worn track crossed a shallow depression filled with 18 inches of mud. The mules' attempt to negotiate this was all but successful, but they came to a compulsory halt just short. No persuasion and certainly no violence would have stirred them. They had done their best and achieved a splendid failure.

From the 23rd to the 27th was a very quiet period. The usual working parties were furnished. A draft of forty-four men arrived, including some we had left behind in England. Lieut. Brocklebank rejoined after undergoing instruction in Adjutant's duties with the 1st Cheshire Regiment. On the 28th we were relieved by the 5th Seaforths and returned to billets in Hénencourt. We had suffered only one casualty, but we here lost the further services of Major Rutherford, the Medical Officer, who was incapacitated by the recent rigours of trench life and was now transferred for duty with the Divisional Field Ambulance. His place was taken temporarily by Captain Titmas, R.A.M.C.

Until the 5th December we followed the usual "rest" routine in these well-tried billets. Much time was spent in removing mud from equipment and clothing. This tenacious element, matter in the wrong place, added considerably to the difficulties of marching. On this day we marched back to trenches and relieved a unit of the 153rd Brigade on the left of "F.1" sector at Aveluy. Three Companies were in the firing line and one in support. The front line was divided into three groups, the spaces in between being impassable owing to mud. The trench in the middle of the salient was badly smashed up by a bombardment a few days previously. Battalion Headquarters were at Lower Donnet. The three Companies in the front line were relieved the following day by two Companies (overstrength) of the 17th Highland Light Infantry, the relieved Companies going into billets in Aveluy. Captain J. Caddy and Lieut. J. A. T. Clarke joined from the third line unit. Captain Caddy had served as Staff Captain of our Brigade until invalided some few months previously and now rejoined for duty. He was succeeded as Staff Captain by Captain J. Fisher. Some shells fell on Aveluy on and around the railway bridge, and one man was wounded.

On the 11th we relieved the 17th Highland Light Infantry in the trenches, where conditions were now exceedingly bad, especially for " A " and " C " Companies. Mud was over the knees in most places. Things were very quiet, accounted for by the fact that the enemy's trenches were in a similar predicament to our own, as reported by one of our reconnoitring patrols under Lance-Corporal Bates. The time was occupied in attempting to clean the trench, and cases of trench feet began to occur through constant standing in the wet.

Captain J. V. Barrow and Lieut. A. Beardsley were here ordered to proceed to England to report to the War Office and left the Battalion, much to our regret. On the 16th we were relieved and marched back to billets in Hénencourt. Here the usual peaceful routine was shattered by a tragedy. Second-Lieut. Ward, whilst demonstrating to a class of beginners in the use of Hand Grenade No. 1, accidentally exploded the bomb, with the result that he was badly wounded and died almost immediately afterwards. One man was killed and thirteen others wounded. Needless to say this event cast a gloom over the remainder of our stay in billets.

Lieut. J. H. C. Gatchell, R.A.M.C., was appointed Medical Officer of the unit in place of Captain Titmas, and forty reinforcements arrived. On the 21st we relieved the 6th Black Watch in Authuille village, with " C " Company in Mound Keep, the time being devoted to cleaning shelters and putting up wire beds. The enemy put over thirty-two shells in the vicinity of Mound Keep, which seemed to be intended for Mac-Mahon's Blockhouse. No shell hit the building and no casualties or damage was done. We marked Christmas Day by moving into the front line in relief of the 4th Loyals, and the Germans shelled Martinsart and killed one of our mules. We were thankful to find the trenches comparatively dry, and after being worked at, habitable. We here lost Major R. P. Little, who was sent to hospital and thence to England, sick. Lieut. E. Spearing had the bad luck to get in the way of a rifle grenade, which he received in the shoulder, and went to the Field Ambulance, wounded. Second-Lieut. Leslie Bowman joined the Battalion from the third line unit.

The trenches were fairly quiet, trench mortars being the chief offenders. Several dud " oil cans " were sent over by " Fritz." Evidence had been accumulating for some time that moves on an unusual scale were being contemplated. This evidence was confirmed when the Brigade was relieved on the 2nd January by the 96th Infantry Brigade, and we marched into billets once more at Hénencourt.

CHAPTER IV.

ARRAS.

ALL this time in France our Brigade had formed part of the 51st (Highland) Division. This apparent anomaly—a Lancashire brigade in a Highland division—arose through paucity of men and the consequent necessity for compression and rearrangement of units in the early days. The unusual association worked remarkably well. The subsequent careers of the two Divisions—the 51st and 55th—on the Western Front, both of which won outstanding reputations, serves but to emphasise the sentiments of respect for a fine Division, which were ours throughout the time we had the unique honour of serving with them. Times were changing, and we were to get back to our own Lancashire formation. What was to be our last stay in Hénencourt was very short, and on the 3rd the Battalion girded itself together and set off on a series of marches, by fairly easy stages, for its new destination. The end of the first day found us at Montigny, and on the second at Coisy, where Second-Lieut. P. J. Blundell joined us. Here we stayed two days, and, continuing our movement further and further west, and further and further away from the din and squalor of the trenches, we passed through delightful country unspoiled by the ravages of war, through La Chaussee, where we stayed one night, until on the 7th we marched into Longpré-les-Corps-Saints, footsore and weary, and not ill-disposed to the long rest which followed.

Henceforward we belonged to the 164th Brigade, 55th (West Lancs.) Division. The process of collection and assimilation of the component parts of a Division —Artillery, Royal Engineers, Infantry and the Auxiliary Services—went on without a pause, under the supervision of the new Divisional Commander, Major-General Sir Hugh Jeudwine, who on closer acquaintance and in the fullness of time came to be known by the

affectionate and not disrespectful appellation " Judy."
The Infantry units comprising the 164th Brigade were
the 4th King's Own, 8th Liverpool (Irish), 4th Loyals
and 5th Lancashire Fusiliers. After a rest and clean
up we began to take stock of our new surroundings. A
sense of exhilaration and freedom from the clogging
discomforts of the trenches prevailed, and we were in
no mood to be critical. Had we been so fault could
have been found with the billets, which should have
been of the best in this rural backwater. Quite clearly
they had been misused and adverse opinion of the
" last lot in " was again freely expressed. They were
probably new arrivals in France, and only experience
would disclose the practical value of the adage " Do
unto others." In putting this disorder to rights we
had to overcome the antagonism of the inhabitants to
English troops caused thereby, and many were the
complaints to be heard and assuaged. A more cordial
atmosphere was eventually established, but the " last
lot in " had bequeathed a legacy of horse-work.

The surrounding country was well adapted for what
followed. Battalion training of a simple and not too
strenuous nature. The land was undulating in a pleasing
way and eminently suited to small tactical schemes.
Here and there were patches of level ground where cere-
monial drill could be practised. The month being
January no crops were endangered, and the weather
for the time of year was excellent. Time was even
found to form a class of equitation for Officers. This
was of the homely variety, and it is not without
humour to review this imposing parade. All the
young gentlemen, not otherwise required for duty,
were mounted on a mixed lot of hairies, limber and
pack animals, those with a little previous knowledge
adopting an attitude of bored toleration to their less
gifted colleagues. This pleasant exercise went on for
some time, but tragedy all but overtook it. Lieut.
Hodkinson had his long legs astride a yellow pack
pony, the pony stumbled, and in falling poor Hodkinson's foot failed to disconnect with the stirrup.
The pony bolted, dragging its rider along the ground,

and it had travelled a score or two yards before it was stopped by the horrified instructor. Hodkinson was unconscious, rather badly injured, and was in hospital for many days before we saw him again. Equitation was discontinued.

There arrived at this time a draft of sixty-three men, the largest to be received so far, also Second-Lieuts. Corless, Myatt, J. Welch and W. B. McCall joined the Battalion from the Third Line Unit, the latter being posted to " D " Company. On the 17th a scheme of attack was well carried out, the Signallers, under Sergeant T. H. Middleton, particularly distinguishing themselves. On the 22nd we were inspected and reviewed by the Brigadier, who was good enough to express himself satisfied. This was a good result considering the small opportunity we had had to practise this exacting ceremony. Captain Tillyard relinquished his appointment as Adjutant and left for duty at Salonica. He was a gifted linguist and his services were needed further afield. He was succeeded by Lieut. H. A. Brocklebank, who now took over the duties of Adjutant. Captain W. D. Barratt left the Battalion to be O.C. at the new Divisional School at Hallencourt, and Captain J. M. Mawson, having been appointed to the Staff at Etaples, was struck off the strength of the Battalion. On the 26th, Lance-Corporal D. Winnicott, " C " Company, proceeded to England, having been granted a Commission in the Sherwood Foresters. On the 29th there was a Divisional concentration march. The Battalion left Longpré at 8 a.m. and reached Hallencourt at 10.45, where the whole Division was reviewed by the Corps Commander, which ordeal having been negotiated successfully, we returned to billets at 2.30 p.m.

Our pleasant stay at Longpré was rapidly drawing to a conclusion. Having received its hall mark from the Corps Commander our newly-formed Division began to bestir itself, and stretch its wings as it were, prior to new flights. On the 30th January, 1916, at 12 noon, we left Longpré for the last time and marched to Berteaucourt. The Commanding Officer having gone on short leave, Major N. E. Barnes was in command of the Battalion at this time. From here we marched to Candas, where we were to have another lengthy stay under new conditions. Captain Wright here rejoined from the Machine Gun Company and took over command of " D " Company, Second-Lieut. Chapman replacing him.

Candas was a rather insignificant village in the back area, and its importance now lay in its suggestion of a portent. The first stirrings were evident of the giant which, in six months' time, was to transform the face of Northern France, and the whole aspect of the war. We were now to be initiated into these beginnings and make acquaintance with a remarkable organization—the R.O.D., or, to be less mysterious, the Railway Operating Division. This marvellous enterprise was run under the ægis of the Royal Engineers, but probably even that distinguished Corps would disclaim full credit for all its activities and achievements. Its personnel must have been largely recruited from those to the manner born, and with the making and running of railways in the blood, as it were. The rate at which these light railways were growing, connecting existing systems, and extending eventually to the very front, was a source of wonder and amazement.

The surroundings of Candas, flat and uninteresting, lent themselves admirably to the service of yet another phenomenon making itself manifest. The Royal Flying Corps, like the Artillery, had been with us from the beginning, but in minute doses, and to see a British aeroplane was an unusual experience. Powerful forces were at work to remedy this deficiency, which before long were to give undisputed supremacy in the air to the Allies. We found an Aerodrome established at Candas and were prepared to pay homage to its novel personnel. But we reckoned without our unwilling hosts ; not only the canteens, but the village estaminets were locked, bolted and barred against the alien. This was a matter which called for instant adjustment. There were infantry before Pontius Pilate, and this proud arm will survive when the odour of petrol has once more been forgotten! We are not aware whether Major Barnes' representations took this trenchant form, but his views eventually prevailed, and a truce was proclaimed.

On the 1st February the Battalion took over fatigue duties from the 9th Inniskilling Fusiliers. These duties were carried out under the direction of the 112th (Railway) Company, R.E., and consisted in constructing a light railway stretching between Candas and Puckevillers. It was hard work, but interesting and not unpleasant. Each day the working parties went out to railhead, which daily extended, taking their mid-day meal with them, and returning to billets at the close of the day's work. The billets were good, the amenities fair, and existence supportable during those halcyon days. Further serious demands on our already lamentably depleted Roll of Officers had now to be met when orders were received for Major Barnes to be attached to G.H.Q. for special duty and for Captain Barratt to proceed to England for munition work. This continued attrition could not in the nature of things conduce to the efficiency and contentment of the Battalion, which now bore visible evidence of these changes, and it is a tribute to the Battalion's innate qualities that these involuntary departures had no lasting ill effects.

This pleasant interlude lasted for a fortnight, when once again rumours of change filled the air. These duly materialised, and on the 15th the Battalion left Candas at 9.30 a.m. and marched to Thieures, a distance of 11 miles, arriving at 1.30 p.m. after a good march, the weather being in our favour. There we went into billets for the night. Leaving Thieures at 9 a.m. on the following morning we set out on the most villainous march it is possible to imagine. The weather was appalling, with continuous storms of rain accompanied by a gale, and it was a limp and sorry crowd that hobbled into Sombrin at 2 p.m. and dissolved from view into billets already prepared to dry itself to the best of the means available. No further moves being contemplated for the present we settled down for some days, these being devoted to Battalion training. Sergeant Adamson was detached to Brigade Headquarters as Instructor at the Brigade Bombing School. Lieut.-Colonel Carleton took over temporary command of the 164th Brigade and the command of the Battalion consequently devolved on Captain J. Caddy. Training continued but was much interfered with by the weather. It was very cold with heavy snow and frost, the roads being in very bad condition. At 3 p.m. the Battalion left Sombrin and moved to Monchiet, only a matter of six miles, but another awful march, due to causes different in character to the last march, but even more trying in their effects. It blew a blizzard and was very cold. The roads were in bad order, very tiring for the men, and nearly impossible for the transport. Lieut. Neill had a terrible time, but eventually got his transport through. We passed other transport hopelessly ditched and during the night sent parties back to help them out of their difficulties. The snow was quite deep. At Monchiet there joined us a taciturn youth who on introduction, emerged as Lieut. Wilson, R.A.M.C., who remained with us as *locum tenens* for Lieut. Gatchell, our Medical Officer, who was now on leave. Lieut. Wilson was to join us permanently at a later date and loom large in the life of the Battalion—but that is anticipating. At 5 p.m. on the 26th February we left Monchiet and marched to the trenches, relieving the 10th Liverpool Scottish in the Blamont and Ravine trenches in front of Bretencourt.

The area in which we now found ourselves formed a portion of the large re-entrant of which the tortured city of Arras was the apex. The lines of trenches fell away from Arras, in a north-westerly direction towards Aubigny and Loos, and in a south-westerly direction towards Blairville and beyond. A great national highway ran arrow-straight from Doullens to Arras, and in moving from Sombrin and Monchiet on the north the Battalion had to cross this highway on its way to the trenches, situated about ten miles to the south-west of Arras. After crossing this highway the land dipped sharply to the village below. The upper portion, being in view of the enemy and subject to his attentions, was traversed by a communication trench which it were well to utilise in daylight. The village, lying snugly at the lower end of this communication trench, rejoiced in at least two names, if not three. Officially it was known as Bretencourt, but was equally well known as Riviére. It was only about a mile from the line, but many of its inhabitants still clung on to their possessions. Owing to its peculiar position it was comparatively safe, but was subject to high angle fire at times, especially from machine guns. Leaving the village the route rose sharply, past the White Chateau occupied by Brigade Headquarters, and so to the last communication trench. This leads to " The Quarry," a ready-made shelter, where Battalion Headquarters and the First Field Dressing Station are located, thence to the front line.

The Battalion held the right sub-sector of the 164th Brigade front, with the 166th Brigade on the right and 165th Brigade on the left. In front was Blairville in German hands. Intervening, and extending for some 200 yards was No Man's Land, in the middle of which was a considerable clump of osiers, in which patrols from both sides were wont to indulge in grim little games of hide and seek.

The enemy was quiet. It was still snowing hard and the trenches were in a very bad state owing to the thaw which had set in. All available men were set to work but this seemed to have very little effect. Material was scarce, and with more snow falling things were serious. Work was incessant and by the 29th there was a little improvement. A few whizz-bangs were sent over by the enemy on the 1st March but did no damage.

Major-General Jeudwine, Commanding 55th Division visited the trenches and was well pleased with the work done by the Battalion. On the 2nd we were relieved by the 8th Liverpool (Irish) and marched back to Monchiet. It was a poor march, the men being fatigued after incessant work and bad weather in the trenches. We rested the following day, occupying the time in much needed cleaning of equipment. Snow commenced to fall at 8 p.m. and continued all through the night. This lay to a great depth next morning and the Battalion was engaged in clearing the roads round Monchiet, working on the Gouy-Beaumetz and Doullens-Arras roads. Second Lieut. Bowman and 7 O.R. proceeded to Wisques for a Lewis Gun Course. Next morning broke very fine and many aeroplanes were about. The roads were in bad condition and the day was again devoted to their improvement. On the 8th we marched back to the trenches and relieved the 8th Liverpools. The trenches were again very bad and much work had to be done. The evening was quiet but there was some little sniping on the 13th and Company Sergeant-Major Gendle was fatally wounded. On the 16th we went into Brigade Reserve in Bretencourt village. Second Lieuts. James Fisher, Keller and Hodkinson here rejoined us, the latter from the Base Hospital after his rough-riding mishap at Longpré. Second Lieuts. Ferns, Thorpe, Lees and McClinton and 43 other ranks also joined. Lieut. H. A. Brocklebank proceeded on leave, and Lieut. W. C. Neill acted as Adjutant.

For the next three months we remained under these conditions, and in the same area. From the Blamont trenches to billets, these alternating between Monchiet, Bretencourt and finally Simoncourt, the transport having for some time been located at the latter village.

It would be churlish to leave Bretencourt and not mention its popular and prosperous estaminet, the Maison des Glaces, the Glass House, admirably managed by three sisters, Marie, Irene and Adele (or was it Eugenie ?). It is ungallant to be remiss with mademoiselle's name, but more than one could assist as an *aide memoire.* One of our young Officers was her *beau cavalier,* and it was a melting sight to see the tender passages between the two. " Monsieur le Bosche " was the somewhat startling endearment applied to our gallant, probably accounted for by the fact that he wore glasses. Alas, Mademoiselle would be distrait when she learnt that her impetuous admirer, headstrong and bold as ever, was so soon to make the supreme sacrifice. The interludes were good, the atmosphere genial, and the wines above reproach. The weather had vastly improved and we were now free from that portion of our troubles. The enemy, and ourselves, were usually quiet, operations being confined to reconnoitring patrols. Reconnoitring on our part had indeed become the standard pastime, and many were the ghostly forays around the Osier Bed, to the wire beyond. These forays were aided and abetted, indeed led by the C.O. Whatever the wisdom of his personal indulgence as a *shikari,* Col. Carleton's practice coincided with his precepts. Emulation was soon forthcoming and Lieut. Clarke emerged as the principal Battalion fire-eater. It became recognised later that no raiding party was complete without Capt. " Jat " Clarke and the incomparable Private " Jerry " Holmes. This taking of gratuitous risks by Col. Carleton was not confined to No Man's Land. From billets in Bretencourt he was wont to canter, attended by Capt. Caddy, out to morning exercise on the sloping field already referred to, through which wound the first communication trench. This was admirably adapted in normal times for putting a blood mare through her beautiful paces, a charming spectacle, and one which may have appealed to the Germans in whose view it was, for they refrained from using it as a target. One of this remarkable man's recipes for successful campaigning was the importance of small things. The Headquarters Mess became transformed under his tutelage and received the admiring soubriquet " The Quarry Grill." For some time it had been clear that we were not to have his services for long, and on the 12th Col. Carleton left to take over Command of the 98th Infantry Brigade, Major G. B. Balfour taking temporary command of the Battalion. On this date, too, Major-General Jeudwine, Commanding 55th Division, made a most thorough inspection of the Battalion.

Talk of impending big events filled the air. We were intrigued by the arrival of new drafts of Officers and men, and we looked amongst these for new faces from the Furness District but these were becoming fewer. Soon we were up to establishment, an unprecedented achievement for us. Stores of all kinds became more plentiful, and were easier to replace when lost or damaged, and there was a general air of expectancy. On the 19th the Battalion left billets at Simoncourt and marched via Berneville, Warlazel and Dainville Achicourt, to the trenches at Agny, and relieved the 6th D.C.L.I. These trenches were situated a few miles to the north-east of Blamont and about four miles south-west of Arras. The prevailing unrest seemed to have permeated the Hun, and there was much trench activity and some casualties on our side. Amongst these, unfortunately, were Second-Lieut. Johnstone and three other ranks on patrol duty wounded by our own outposts. This Officer had previously captured two Germans from a German patrol.

On the 25th Major J. L. Swainson, D.S.O., a regular Officer of the D.C.L.I. arrived and took over Command of the Battalion. On the 12th July we were relieved by the Liverpool Scottish and marched to Barly, where for four days the Battalion underwent training with a view to an offensive. On the 16th we took over Blamont trenches once more, and on the 20th left Bretencourt for the last time, being relieved by a Battalion of the Northumberland Fusiliers, and marched to Simoncourt.

CHAPTER V.

THE SOMME.

K ITS were now reduced to the required minimum. Surplus kit was stacked and laid aside—with confidence this time that they would be available on the return of less hectic times. G.S. wagons were laden and limbers filled up to their limit, and the Battalion started off on another pilgrimage, its ultimate destination as yet unknown, but only one conclusion could be drawn from the thorough examination of equipment, and the issue of trench maps delineating the battle-front of the Somme. We made Sombrin on the first day after a tiring and dusty march. On the 22nd July the personnel of the Battalion were conveyed by motor bus to Berneuil, the transport moving independently by road. Here we practised the attack by sectional rushes. Before daylight had set in on the 25th the Battalion was on the march, shaping its course through Fienvillers to Candas where other troops, battle-stained and cheerful, laughed at us through the mud and filth which days of incessant fighting had imprinted on their faces. It was the first visible sign of the great offensive.

We entrained at Candas and crawled slowly away past Montrelet and St. Ouen, following the beautiful valley of the Nievre. Optimistic chatterers maintained that we were now pursuing a course directly opposite to that which ought to take us to the front. They did not know, however, that this branch line united with the main railroad from Abbeville to Albért. And the crossing of the viaduct over the Somme marshes soon brought us to the trunk line leading to the heart of hostilities. To our disappointment the train passed through the fine station of Amiens without stopping, the market gardens slipped by, the little vignettes of Senegalese troops became a blur, Corbie of old acquaintance faded from view, and at 2 o'clock we steamed into railhead, Mericourt-Ribemont.

Those of us who had known Méricourt of old were amazed at the change. Then it had been a sleepy little station with a few sidings and a tent or two for the accommodation of prospective *permissionaires.* Now it was the busy centre of all the traffic in men and material feeding the firing line in the sector of Albért. Immense stores of provisions and endless piles of ammunition lay stacked ready for transport. German prisoners, mostly unshaven, were engaged in road mending, or were lazily watching the new troops. Under a blazing sun we marched out of the station. Buire-sur-Ancre showed unmistakable signs of activity. Tired men were dragging themselves along the hot, dusty road, traces of recent fighting plain upon their faces. A few attempted to smile. Sweat ran down and grooved the dirt upon their foreheads and cheeks. Many lacked full equipment. Battalions came out under the command of subalterns, careworn and ageing. Limbers and wagons were rushing up towards the line with food for the men and ammunition for the guns. In happy contrast to the stricken remnants returning from battle were our fresh troops pouring in as reinforcements.

From Méricourt we marched to Méaulte, near Albért, where the Town Major had a particularly trying experience in accommodating Battalion after Battalion in a very restricted area. Confusion at such a time and place, however, was unavoidable. We now formed part of the 13th Corps, Fourth Army. On the 26th we marched to Happy Valley, a comparatively quiet backwater, and took over bivouacs from a Battalion of the 8th Brigade, 3rd Division. Here four days were spent in training under Company arrangements, including much-needed bathing parades to Bray-sur-Somme. There was also an overdue presentation of decorations by Brigadier-General Edwards. There had been a good many individual exploits, thoroughly meriting recognition, and, indeed, recommended for such, which were met with disapproval by the authorities on the ground that the time was "inopportune," and it was not until many more months had passed that decorations began to flow with more facility. An enemy aeroplane dropped bombs on the valley, but there were no casualties amongst our men.

On the night of 30th/31st July the Battalion marched north and took over trenches on a line running north and south between Trones Wood and Guillemont, relieving remnants of the 30th Division. In taking up position we were heavily shelled, losing Second-Lieut. Lincey and three other ranks killed and twelve wounded. Our artillery bombarded heavily all day, and we spent the day digging in, including a shallow German trench in their old line. The immensity of the push was now apparent to us, and our eyes opened in astonishment at the awful havoc of the guns. We, who had seen over twelve months' service, astonished! A giant of steel seemed to have ridden over the proud German defences. Villages were wiped completely out of existence—Fricourt, Mametz, Carnoy, Maricourt, Montauban, all a tumbled heap of rubble; woods were laid waste. Saddest of all there was not a blade of green grass visible. Trenches were everywhere blown out of recognition. In every direction disused gun pits with piles of empty shell cases showed how the artillery had advanced. Disrupted sandbags littered the broken earth. A poignant reminder that victory is not purchased without cost lay in the newly-delved earth, where blue flags were fluttering over the dead.

The transport lay in bivouac in what had been German lines between Fricourt and Maricourt. From this point of vantage much of the terrible drama was visible. Not an inch of ground but was covered by war material and troops resting. Mametz Road presented an unparalleled scene of activity. Never for an instant was it idle. There were up-roads and down-roads everywhere. Ammunition, food, guns went up the one in constant streams; wounded and fatigued men, empty ammunition and ration limbers, came rolling back on the other. Whenever any portion of the road showed signs of wear, either by shell-fire or natural attrition, gangs of men from labour battalions set to work, metalling and restoring. These men were nearly all over age. They had none of the hot glory of conflict. To them fell no stirring battle honours. Yet who but must admire the spirit that sent these gallant veterans into the zone of shell-fire.

The view of the fighting from the actual front was, of necessity, local. But here a much broader outlook was possible. Looking down Mametz valley—" Death Valley " as it was colloquially known—towards Montauban on the left and Trones Wood on the right centre, a mile away, the immense superiority of our guns in the first place struck the observer. The guns were everywhere, " ubique " indeed. They were literally wheel to wheel. Recalling those dark days of 1915, when we asked for support, and asked in vain, it made one's heart rejoice, with a strange exultation to see those inexhaustible stacks of shells and to hear the incessant roaring of the guns.

And then one could not fail to be impressed with our mastery of the air. How effectively the enemy had been blinded became daily more obvious. The hum of aircraft rung in the ears as the guns slackened. All day long the droning battleplane wheeled over the scene of carnage. Reconnoitring planes flew backwards and forwards with information of enemy masses, train movements and gun positions. The more humble contact planes hung a few hundred feet over the advancing troops and reported progress to the artillery. They flew unperturbed over the avalanche of our own shells. Whenever an objective was attained by our infantry coloured flares ascended and the contact aeroplane immediately conveyed the intelligence to the gunners, who lengthened their range and prepared the ground for further advance.

Not only in aeroplanes were we seemingly supreme. Observational work by aircraft was necessarily hasty and brief. It was the captive balloon that supplied the more detailed and continuous information. These balloons were connected to earth by telephone. As many as twenty-five could be counted swinging lazily in the breeze. Indeed, the increasing salient of our battle front, as we bit deeper and deeper into the German defences, could be gauged by the wide crescent of these aerial outposts.

Not only above, but underneath, had this amazing tornado passed. Our human moles had burrowed with an uncanny sense of direction right underneath those ingeniously contrived German subterranean passages. They had prepared—with an immense amount of patience, self-sacrifice and danger, daring not only detection by the enemy, but the far more insidious peril of poison gas—mines beside which those at La Boisselle shrunk into pettiness. And then, in a moment, by the mere pressure of an electric button, in a mighty convulsion they had overwhelmed all those galleries and caverns where the enemy was cowering under the avalanche of our shells.

" Death Valley " then was now the centre of this hellish activity. Blinded as they were the Germans poured a prodigal amount of ammunition into it, and they had their own old positions ranged to a nicety. And it is easy to understand how effective such a mass of fire could be, when this was the only avenue by which rations could be brought up to the infantry or ammunition for the guns. One would see a G.S. waggon, pair of horses and driver, careering down this satanic road with ammunition, a stray shell, and blankness—nothing to mark the event but an additional shell-hole, which the devoted labour corps hurried out like solicitous ants to investigate and repair. In spite of the frightful punishment the enemy were undergoing at our hands, inaction could never be laid to their charge. Each day saw their defences, so seriously threatened, grow more formidable. Their pioneers were tireless. Their " Betontruppen," specialists in the erection of concrete machine-gun emplacements, or " strong-points," and their " Hollenbankommandos," for the construction of dugouts, were organizing a newly-formed system of trenches on a scale of great magnitude, and with the invaluable accessories of strong points. Trenches, wired and traversed, emerged in a single night. The favourable features of the ground were everywhere transformed into miniature fortresses of amazing strength, from whose loop-holed bastions machine-guns in countless numbers pushed their deadly muzzles.

The sector of trenches occupied by us lay on the extreme right of the British position, before Guillemont. On our right were the 156th Regiment of Infantry, 10th Corps, French Army, and on our left the 8th Liverpools. Guillemont was marked for early attack, but the time was not yet. Artillery activity on both sides was continuous. The enemy appeared to be nervous. At 8.30 p.m. on 1st August " B " Company attacked an advanced German strongpoint with one platoon. This platoon was hung up and forced to retire, owing to enemy barrage, which was very severe. At 8.45 p.m. another platoon went forward under Second-Lieut. A. J. Brockman and was completely successful. We had previously dislodged the enemy with Stokes Mortar bombs, and as they were retreating in large numbers (apparently the enemy was massing for an attack) our artillery barrage caught them and inflicted very severe casualties on them. Our casualties were slight, Second-Lieut. Rudduck being wounded. In this brisk encounter communication by telephone lasted for exactly an hour under a most severe and accurate enemy shelling. In the early morning of 3rd August the Battalion was relieved by the 4th Loyals and moved into Brigade Reserve, in Dublin and Casement trenches, in front of Maricourt, that is, to the rear of the Mametz valley.

The enemy shelled the left of our trenches but did not cause any damage. We found some fatigue parties, including two for the front line. On the night of the 4th we were relieved by the 5th Liverpools, of the 165th Brigade, and proceeded to bivouacs south of Carnoy and west of Bronfay Farm. The weather was very hot and the next three days were spent quietly with bayonet fighting, physical drill and bathing parades. At 6 p.m. on the 7th sudden orders were received, and at 8.15 p.m. the Battalion left bivouacs and proceeded to trenches near Arrow Head Copse, in sector south of Trones Wood and Guillemont Road. There was an awful congestion of troops in the Sunken Road, but, fortunately, no shelling, and the Battalion did not have a single casualty during the relief, which was completed by 1 a.m., when preparations were made for the attack on Guillemont.

The order of battle from right to left was " D," " A," " B " and " C " Companies. At 3.45 a.m. on 8th August the first line, consisting of two platoons of each Company, crept out in front of the advanced trench, at the same time the remainder of the Battalion occupied the advanced trench. At 4.10 the first line advanced a short way and waited four minutes. Second line left the trench and took up a position twenty yards in rear of the first line. The second line was closely followed by two platoons of the 4th Loyals as carrying party. At 4.15 the enemy placed a very violent barrage of artillery fire (shrapnel) on the fire trench. The first and second lines crept forward closer to our own barrage to escape enemy fire. At 4.20 the Battalion went forward again and the first line immediately came under heavy bomb fire. This was absolutely unexpected, caused heavy casualties, and the attack was arrested. The enemy then opened very heavy machine-gun and rifle fire, which caught the second line as it came up to reinforce the first line.

Further advance being impossible, owing to uncut wire, the Battalion retired out of bombing distance from the German trench and started to dig in, fifty yards in front of our original trench. These operations occupied twenty minutes. The enemy maintained a very heavy barrage of shrapnel on the Sunken Road during the whole of this time. The only means of communication during this time, with the exception of one Company, to which the telephone wire was intact, was by runner. Communication with the Battalion on the left was completely lost. It was ascertained that this Battalion was reported to be in the village of Guillemont, and it was intended to make an attempt to get into touch with their right. Stokes Mortars were brought up and were ordered to destroy the barricade on the Sunken Road leading to Guillemont, with the idea of attacking and taking this point and which would have enabled an advance on the left to be covered. There was a great deal of delay in bringing up the Stokes Mortar ammunition, the difficulties of communication were great, and it made it extremely hard for orders to reach their destination. This delay gave the enemy a long period of rest, which was unfavourable to the success of any further enterprise.

The Stokes Mortars bombarded the barricade, but were not successful in damaging it. It was intended that a bombing party should assault at 12 noon, but the situation was seen to be quite hopeless for the success of such an enterprise.

Our artillery, in the meantime, kept up an intermittent bombardment for a long period. They were firing very short and our front line had to be cleared. It was with the greatest difficulty that the artillery were informed of this, which caused some casualties to the Battalion. It was decided that any further attack was impracticable and efforts were concentrated on improving the present position as far as possible and to render it easily defensible in the event of any hostile offensive. The Battalion was by this time greatly reduced in numbers and was also fatigued by the strain of the heavy fighting. There was a shortage of Officers. It was not known what had happened to the Battalion on the left, and although all effort was made to ascertain their position no information was obtainable. It was impossible to obtain accurate information, which made the situation worse. The remainder of the night was spent in trying to collect wounded, improve our original position, and clear the battlefield. At 3.55 a.m. on the 9th we were relieved by the 10th Liverpool Scottish and proceeded, sorely stricken and almost unmanned by the terrific strain of the recent fighting and the shambles around us, to bivouac south-west of Carnoy.

The Battalion arrived in small parties. Stragglers came in during the day. Captain Huthwaite, of the charmed life, wandering about like a distracted shepherd looking for his flock, collected a number of these and brought them in. A roll call was made with lamentable results, disclosing eight Officers killed, including the Commanding Officer, and nine wounded; 254 other ranks, including 48 killed and 206 wounded and missing. The Officers were :—

Killed.	*Wounded.*
Lieut.-Col. J. L. Swainson, D.S.O.	Capt. Neill.
	2nd-Lt. Welch.
Capt. R. D'A. Morrell.	2nd-Lt. Ferns.
Capt. A. A. Wright.	2nd-Lt. Withey.
2nd-Lt. Hodkinson.	2nd-Lt. Clark.
2nd-Lt. Brockman.	2nd-Lt. S. F. Walker.
2nd-Lt. Lawson.	2nd-Lt. Wilcock.
2nd-Lt. L. Metcalf.	2nd-Lt. Jackson.
2nd-Lt. Hilton.	2nd-Lt. Metcalfe.

The loss of the Commanding Officer was a stunning blow. Although he had only been with us six weeks his influence on the Battalion was marked and beneficent. We found ourselves guided by a firm hand, directed with understanding. It was not given to every regular Officer at that time to see eye to eye with the aspirations and latent qualities of the Territorial Army. Captain Jackson, our late Adjutant, had possessed this rare faculty and was ready to admit and proclaim that in some essential military respects, of which trench-digging was only one, the Territorial Army could more than hold its own. Colonel Swainson was another with this gift of insight, and with his regular experience, his knowledge of what to do, and perhaps more important, what not to do, the Battalion seemed set for a period of what can best be termed happy soldiering, when he met his untimely end.   The Command now devolved upon Major G. B. Balfour.

For many days no recollection of these horrors was permitted to diminish the enthusiasm of the Division. Concerts were held nightly.   On the bare slopes near Carnoy the infantry, worn out by their recent trials, engaged themselves in innocent relaxation.

The theatre party of the Division, under our own Lieut. Leslie, addressed themselves to their congenial offices with a diligence no less justified of the times than it was deserving of support.   Blood had freely flowed and would flow again as freely.   In the meantime no dejection of spirits must be allowed to usurp the place of contentment and good cheer.   The guns were still ranged solidly against the enemy and pulverising his trenches.   His own artillery, admittedly well-handled, was redoubling its opposition.   More and more troops, eager to win renown, and excited by the unwonted activity, were pouring up towards the line.   Defeated and despairing, the Germans, stung to a paroxysm of frenzy, were hurling themselves on their lost positions.   Forfeitures of ground, privations unproclaimed, renunciation of hope, submission and subjugation—all these things they had been taught to abhor.   And now, as we forced them to accept adversity, they resisted with fierce courage.

The weather continued very hot.   On the following day the remnants of the Battalion paraded by companies for inspection, re-organisation and checking deficiencies in equipment.   Major-General Jeudwine, commanding the Division, inspected us and cheered us by his very austerity.   A working party of one Officer and 70 other ranks went into the front line to dig forward communication trenches.   They were heavily shelled by enemy artillery but only two casualties were caused.   We observed one of our forward trench balloons break away from its moorings and sail away over the enemy lines.   The occupant was equal to the occasion and got out of his difficulties by the aid of a parachute.   On the 14th we left bivouacs at Carnoy and marched to Méricourt with the Brigade, via Sand Pit, Meaulte, Ville-sur-Ancre Treux, the transport travelling under Brigade arrangements via Bray-sur-Somme.

The Battalion rested in billets in Méricourt, the time being spent in refitting, reorganisation and steady drill. Bathing, too, received attention, the weather being still very hot. A draft of 100 other ranks from the 3/10th Manchester Regiment joined us and proved a good lot of men. For the present the Division was not to be re-engaged on the Somme, and at 4 a.m. on the 19th the Battalion paraded at Méricourt Station and entrained for Abbeville, arriving at 11.30 a.m. Time did not admit of the hoped-for coffee and omelette at the "Bull's Head," and at 11.40 we were off again on the march, over the bridge leading to the south side of the Somme, through Rouvroy and Cambron, until at 4 p.m. we arrived in billets at Lambercourt.

We shall never forget that sweet corner of France. The fresh profusion of green grass and yellow stubble, the prodigal wealth and variety of arboreal treasures with abundant foliage, fruit trees laden with their gracious burden. The scattered houses of the village, nestling within bowers of roses and other sweet-smelling flowers, a thin blue reek ascending from some chimney in a thatched roof. Sharply and suddenly contrasted with the din and horror we had left so recently these quiet scenes brought tears to the eyes and a sense of realisation that a beneficent Power was still in charge of human destiny.

A cavalry regiment had been dislodged in order that the P.B.I. might have a fleeting respite in this corner of paradise. Whence they had departed was a matter of conjecture, probably to another delectable billet, as their turn had not yet come in the maelstrom. For ten days the Battalion enjoyed the seclusion of this peaceful retreat. The time was given over to platoon training, whilst drafts of reinforcements continued to arrive. On the 23rd all Officers and N.C.O.'s attended a lecture at Brigade Headquarters, given by General Jeudwine, on the recent operations. A pleasing feature at this time was the special short leave granted to small parties to St. Valery-sur-Somme and Tréport. These were delightful little watering-places on the estuary of the Somme, and it was whispered that the delights of a casino awaited visitors to either place. Plans were in preparation to extend these privileges to Paris, when the bolt fell from the blue and the Battalion again turned its face to the east.

At 11.15 p.m. on August 29th we left Lambercourt in light marching order, the men's packs having been despatched separately by motor-lorry, and marched via Cambron, Rouvroy, St. Marguerite, Mareuil, Bray-les-Mareuil and Duncq to Pont Remy, where we arrived at 5 a.m. and had breakfast. Entraining and leaving Pont Remy at 8 o'clock we passed through Amiens and Corbie and arrived at Méricourt-Ribemont at 11.40 a.m., on the inner edge of hostilities once more. The Battalion moved to a point adjoining the main Albert-Corbie road where billets in tents and hutments awaited us. The weather was now unfavourable. Ten Officer reinforcements joined from the base. Battalion training occupied us during our stay in billets, and at midnight on September 7th we moved into trenches in Montauban Alley, where we were in Brigade reserve, relieving the 1st South Staffords. On the 10th the Battalion moved up and helped to man our front line trenches in Delville Wood, after the failure of a previous attack. Here the Companies were all split up and it was difficult to acquire accurate information. At 6 p.m. orders were received from Brigade to carry out an attack by surprise at 5.15 a.m. on to Hop Alley and German trenches on the western side of Delville Wood. This attack was duly carried out with " D " Company on left flank, " A " and " B " Companies in the centre, and " C " Company on the right. All ranks were dead tired and there was no dash in the attack, which failed directly the Germans opened with machine gun and rifle fire. Our casualties in this encounter were not very heavy, but Lieut. E. Spearing, commanding " D " Company, and Second-Lieut. G. R. Glenie, Lewis-Gun Officer, were both missing and were later found to have been killed in action. The remainder of the 11th and 12th was spent in holding the front line, which was heavily shelled, causing heavy casualties. We were relieved by the 8th King's Royal Rifles and returned to bivouac at Becourt.

On the 13th the Battalion marched to Ribemont and bivouacked in canvas shelters. Four officers reported here for duty, including Captain R. Gardner, who rejoined the Battalion on recovery from his unlucky adventure with a Very light some months previously, and Second-Lieut. T. H. Middleton, having been appointed to a commission from Sergeant-Signaller. From Ribemont to Buire, where we found comfortable billets for both officers and men, and where we saw 850 German prisoners being marched to the rear. The 17th, being Sunday, we attended a Brigade Church Parade, when the Padre's sermon was based on St. Peter "warming himself at the fire," with personal reminiscences of training in England during the early days of the war. From Buire to Becordel, where we went into bivouacs in drenching rain near Mametz prisoners' camp.

The new bivouacs were devoid of any comfort whatsoever. A few shelters were improvised for the night, but very few enjoyed satisfactory shelter. Funkholes were dug at irregular intervals, in case the enemy opened artillery fire. In the murky and rainy night, when men arrived in driblets from heavy working parties, covered with mud from head to foot, limping with fatigue, and hungry as only men are hungry when much strenuous labour is required, there were often no means of showing these poor wretches the many pitfalls that lay in their path. Stumbling over the tangle of brushwood and falling into the soft oozy mud lining the bottom of the funk-holes, I have heard them groping blindly for shelter, swearing roundly at everything. But I have never failed to hear them *sing* when, under equal conditions, they have found a few inches of tarpaulin ready to shield them from the bitter cold, or a scattering of straw to serve as their pallet. One is apt to grumble at home over little things. Let him not grumble till he has passed a night under such conditions as these.

Our front line had advanced considerably, and the next area of operations was Longueval and Flers, well in front of Delville Wood. After Holy Communion on the 24th the Battalion proceeded to occupy reserve trenches known as Green Trench and King's Walk. Officers reconnoitred the lines of approach to Flers, and Second-Lieut. Beazley was wounded. Our bombardment developed in severity, and on the 26th orders were received to move forward, three platoons to strong points at the end of Cove Alley and one company and one platoon to Smoke Trench, while Battalion Headquarters moved up to east of Flers.

On the 27th the 55th Division resumed active operations. The 8th Liverpool Irish were detailed to assault and capture Gird and Gird Support trenches, and the 4th King's Own to furnish the fifth wave in attack. Parties carried R.E. material for making strong points to Grove Alley and Gird Support trenches. The trench was easily captured by the 8th Liverpools, and the carrying parties carried out their duties successfully and without casualties. These parties then occupied a position on Factory Corner—Gueude-court Road, keeping in touch on the left with the 4th King's Own. Arrangements were made later to relieve the 8th Liverpool Irish in the captured trenches. Several casualties were sustained in a bombardment subsequent to the attack. At 2 a.m. on the 28th the 4th King's Own took over Gird and Gird Support trenches from the 8th Liverpools. The trenches were heavily bombarded during the day by the enemy. Three patrols with Lewis guns were sent out to locate the German position and harass a working party which had been seen earlier in the morning. At 2 a.m. on the 29th the Battalion was relieved in the trenches by the Royal West Surreys and re-assembled at Mametz, where a *contretemps* all but ended in minor disaster. The Quartermaster had been handed over a paragon of bivouacs in the form of tents, one of the best we had experienced, and was keeping watch and ward over this treasure, when he was horrified to see a battalion of New Zealanders descend upon him like the Assyrians of old, or the plague of locusts, and take possession. Protests from a mere Quartermaster of Infantry were met with airy nonchalance. Other and prompt steps had to be taken. Olivette was saddled and made short work of the journey to Brigade Headquarters, where a sympathetic Staff Captain got busy, wires were set sizzling, and the anxious Quartermaster eventually had the satisfaction of seeing these unconventional soldiers march out of one end of the camp as his precious Battalion hobbled in at the other, happily unconscious of their narrow escape from homelessness. We moved thence to very crowded billets in Dernacourt.

This was to be the close of our memorable association with the Somme, for the present, at any rate. The approach of winter placed an insuperable barrier on hopes of much further advance. Progress had been definite, if it had not met the most sanguine expectations, but the courageous tenacity and marvellous organization of the enemy revealed the magnitude of the task yet to be completed.

CHAPTER VI.

Ypres.

FOR the present we were not to be re-engaged upon the Somme, but, transported to Longpré, were moved into quarters for the night of October 1st at Bouchon. The following day we entrained at Longpré and moved to the north. In the early afternoon we passed through Abbeville. The tented dunes of Etaples swarmed with reinforcements. As darkness descended we entered the region of the flats of Flanders. The coast line receded. Boulogne and Calais were left far behind. St. Omer and Haze-brouck were before us. Soon these, too, were swallowed up in the night. At midnight we detrained at Hopoutre and marched away. As dawn was breaking officers and men threw themselves down to snatch a little sleep in billets already provided at Poperinghe, ten miles west of Ypres. From here, after bathing parade, the Battalion marched to "O" Camp, a few miles nearer Ypres and just off the main Poperinghe-Ypres road. This camp consisted of the usual pattern army huts, nearly new, and, being weather proof, provided excellent accommodation, and were much appreciated by the men after their rough experiences of the past two months.

This, then, was our first introduction to the Ypres salient. Many times in the early days we had hovered on its brink, and it seemed strange that we should be only now making its close acquaintance, eighteen months afterwards. Although we felt ourselves a little disappointed with our renewed acquaintance with the Flemish fogs and flats, we gradually adapted ourselves to the changed conditions. A year had made a vast difference in our powers of appreciation. Casting back to those grim days of Festubert there stood out in bold relief pools rotting with dead, trenches constructionally weak, and an enemy gunnery the mastery of which was denied us for many a long

day to come.   But the passing of twelve months had
shown us, week by week, such striking improvements
that there was now no limit to our confidence.   All
these things reacted favourably on our outlook.   Our
fickle minds recalled only the monotony of the rolling
Picard uplands.   They were now touched by the
vision of a new beauty.

For ten days the Battalion enjoyed immunity from
the strain of exacting work.   The usual parades were
held to preserve discipline and efficiency.   After the
routine of daily parades and inspections it was customary for a few of us to ride or cycle into Poperinghe,
about six kilometres distant.   Poperinghe was the
point of convergence for the military in the Ypres
salient, as Béthune was for the La Bassée sector,
Doullens for Arras, and Amiens for the Somme.

One of the first things to meet the eye was the
prominence given to " Gas Alarms."   A large notice
was exhibited on a building in the main square, where
the road to Ypres left the town, which read " Wind
Dangerous " or " Wind Safe."   Otherwise its amenities bore comparison with towns of greater pretensions.
There was an attractive Officers' Club, established
in a spacious building named Talbot House, after its
founder, Colonel Talbot, of an ancient lineage and a
staff officer.   Here resided the Padre, the Rev.
" Tubby " Clayton, who afterwards was to render
Talbot House famous as the orginal home of its
illustrious offspring, " Toc H."   This club had the
air of quiet decorum associated with its kind, and
it was held by the irreverent that any shell—from
which, alas, Poperinghe was not immune—from the
German " Long Tom," more impetuous than its
fellows and ill-advised enough to invade those awful
precincts, would shrivel to impotence in its frigid
atmosphere.   This was, of course, uncharitable, but
the painful fact must be recorded that the younger
element preferred the freer delights of Skindle's and
Kiki's, two restaurants whose air of gay animation
made an irresistible appeal to war-worn youth.   Here
the unheard of luxuries of fresh fish and even oysters

were included in a generous menu. These arrived daily, we were informed, by canal from Dunkerque. Here also was established the Divisional Concert Party, which had now attained a high standard of efficiency in the exacting art of entertainment. These played nightly as to the manner born to crowded audiences, whose plaudits testified to the quality of the entertainment and their own high spirits. One of these artists was a young imp of the 4th Loyals, who made up in startling fashion as " Poppy Poperinghe."

The appointment of Lieut.-Colonel G. B. Balfour to the command of the Battalion, which he had held since the death of Lieut.-Colonel Swainson, and that of Major H. A. Brocklebank as second-in-command, was here confirmed. The appointment of Adjutant was vacant about this time and was not filled permanently until Sergeant-Major J. Way was commissioned and appointed on December 23rd, 1916. Lieut. Mudie held the acting appointment for one period of the interim and probably another officer, whose name does not emerge.

On the 13th the Battalion was inspected by Brigadier-General Stockwell and was complimented on its turn-out. The Brigadier took the opportunity of presenting decorations and medals—the Military Cross to Company Sergeant-Major R. A. Williams, the Distinguished Conduct Medal to Private C. Milton, and Military Medals to Second-Lieut. T. H. Middleton, Sergeants H. W. Percival and P. Stalker and Privates W. Nicholson and H. Jackson. At 5.15 p.m. on the 14th we marched to Brandhoek Station and entrained for Ypres, arriving at 7.30. Here we went into quite good billets in the town—or what remained of it— some in the ramparts and the remainder in the school.

Of all the ghostly and melancholy ruins along the western front Ypres stands out almost unchallenged. Right from the beginning it had borne the brunt of the enemy's insensate fury, and withstood it. It still stood four square to the foe and marked the eastern boundary of that tiny strip of Belgium, still held by the gallant Belgian army on our left and ourselves. The deplorable ruin of its once beautiful structure bore evidence of the cost of its retention. The square and its surrounding buildings, including the ancient and lovely Cloth Hall, were a heap of powdered rubble, with here and there a stark stump of wall and an arched window still surviving. These maimed remnants were periodically repulverised by senseless bombardment by the enemy even as a dog returns to its vomit. I have known no more eerie feeling than that experienced when crossing this desolate square on a quiet night. Many of the houses in the remoter suburbs were less damaged, and their cellars made excellent shelters when the Hun carried out his frequent bombardments of this martyred town. The civilian population had long been evacuated.

The trench system was divided into two sectors, the left, or Potijze, and the right, or Railway Wood. The latter was approached by way of the Menin Gate and road, past the notorious Hell Fire Corner, and over the railway connecting Ypres and Menin in normal times. The trenches were fair and there were some good dugouts.

The communication trenches leading up to the front line, however, left something to be desired. These were named West Lane and Mud Lane (afterwards re-named Beek Trench, so as not to damage the morale of reinforcements !).

On the right of this sub-sector were two or three craters left by previous mine operations, and the width of these craters represented the distance between the enemy and ourselves, who manned the opposite lips. A deathly silence usually reigned at this point, the slightest movement or sound being audible on either side.

Still further to the right the line was incomplete. A line of " grouse butts " connected it with the Menin Road (the left-hand boundary of the Division on our right). These " grouse butts " were not held during the day but were occupied at night by Lewis Gun Sections and carefully patrolled.

When visiting these posts one night Captain R. Gardner was "captured" by the Division on the right and marched down to their Battalion Head Quarters so that his identity might be established!

At 6.30 p.m. on the 15th the Battalion moved off by platoons and took over trenches in the right sub-sector at Railway Wood. On our left were the 8th Liverpool Irish and on our right the New Zealanders. The trenches needed repair and there was not much rest for the Companies. There was some activity by the enemy, who threw over many trench mortar bombs. One of these made a direct hit on one of our cookhouses, killing one man and wounding another. On the other hand our snipers reported having bagged three Bosche. On the night of the 19th we were relieved and marched back to our old billets in Ypres.

Twelve new officers, from the Lancashire Fusiliers, now joined us—Captains F. H. Williamson and F. C. Slater and Lieuts. W. R. Pattinson, G. Topham, J. H. Simpson, Second-Lieuts. C. W. Ford, J. C. Alexander, R. A. Mudie, J. S. Patterson, R. Willett, J. Pearson and A. T. Sheahan. Companies were re-organised—Captain Gardner to " A " Company, Captain Slater " B," Captain Huthwaite " C," and Captain Williamson " D " Company. Half the Battalion were moved into the prison along with Battalion Head-quarters. These billets were not bad, but cold. Working parties were provided nightly for duty in the trenches. On the 23rd we moved into trenches in the Potijze sector on the left. The weather was bad and much labour was expended in pumping water out of the trenches and in reveting. Everyone wore gum boots, water being over the duck boards. The enemy was fairly quiet, but five of our men were hit by shell fire.

The Brigadier was insistent upon repairs to trenches and to wire, and upon obtaining command of No Man's Land by constant patrolling. Patrols visited the ruins of Oder House, situated between the lines, and examined (from a respectful distance) a salient in the German lines known as Kaiser Bill.

On the 27th we were relieved and went back to billets in Ypres, moving thence on the 30th to Elverdinghe, a little further to the rear, where we found good billets for all, Battalion Headquarters being accommodated in the chateau. Here a Defence Scheme was in operation, and working parties were provided to maintain the trench system and strong points, and test-manning of these points was carried out periodically. Lieut.-Colonel G. B. Balfour went on leave and Major H. A. Brocklebank took over temporary command. Captain H. Y. Huthwaite reported sick and was transferred to England and later to the Indian Army, greatly to the Battalion's loss.

The campaign now took the form of monotonous routine, life alternating between the many camps round Ypres—" C," " D," " O " and " P," and quite good they were.

When out of the line the Battalion found a great many working parties for the laying of telephone cables from the Reserve Areas up to Ypres, especially round Machine Gun Farm.

Ypres itself, with an occasional turn in the front line trenches at Potijze, St. Julien and Railway Wood. The Higher Command were curious to learn the composition and quality of the enemy in front, and for some time a raiding party of the 4th King's Own had been organising and rehearsing a sudden descent on the enemy. These rehearsals were very practical in their value. A replica, as far as possible, of the enemy's position to be raided was marked out by tapes on the practice ground and times and distances were carefully noted. On December 21st there was a full and final rehearsal at " O " Camp, and the raiding party of 200, under Captain J. A. T. Clarke, were inspected by the Commander-in-Chief, Sir Douglas Haig. On the evening of the 22nd the raiders dined in the large hall of the Prison in Ypres, and at 1.30 a.m. on the 23rd they were armed and inspected prior to their departure for the operation. With their faces and hands blacked to minimise refraction of light and to facilitate recognition of their own side during the actual raid, they looked a grim lot. The raiders commenced to leave the Prison in small groups at 3.15 a.m. and journeyed to the " jumping-off place," a ditch running north and south in the St. Julien sub-sector.

Their objective was to enter the German trenches and penetrate to the Cameron support trench, with a view to killing or taking prisoners and thus securing identification. At 5.25 a.m., under a very effective artillery barrage, our men entered the enemy trenches according to plan and penetrated as far as the support line. These trenches were very badly knocked about by our barrage and, unfortunately, no prisoners were taken and no identifications were obtained, the Bosche evidently having abandoned his trenches when the bombardment commenced. Our casualties were two officers, Second-Lieuts. Smith and Hart, wounded, two other ranks killed, three missing, and thirty wounded. This was a brisk and well carried out minor action, and if the main result was disappointing, this was due to the discretion of the Hun and perhaps defective preliminary action on our part. Registering and preliminary bombardment having been carried out by us for a week the fact of the raid had been effectively advertised. Surprise methods which were adopted later were more successful. Sergeant M. Caddy was killed—a good experienced N.C.O. and a loss to the Battalion.

We must not omit to devote a little space to the remarkable personality of the Corps Commander. The ubiquity of General Sir Aylmer Hunter-Weston was phenomenal. He was fond of touring the front line, and on coming to a sentry post, to mark his estimate of the importance of that duty, he would stand in front of the bewildered sentry, saying, " I, your Corps Commander, salute you," and, suiting the action to the word, did actually give the sentry a most ceremonious salute. He was keen on researches on the roofs of and behind cookhouses, while at Battalion parade inspection he made men take off their boots, and exposed officers' ignorance of the " innards " of a water-cart. That legend should gather round his name is not surprising. He was a fine officer whose sterling work in France commenced with a Brigade in the original British Expeditionary Force.

Wintry weather of the severest description now gripped the land. Snow was frequent and frost so intense that anything liquid was quickly turned to ice. This condition persisted to the end of March, when there was a welcome break.

The Division was relieved early in January, 1917, by the 39th Division. The 165th and 166th Brigades went out at once, but the 164th Brigade, to which we belonged, was kept back in Reserve in view of a possible attack against the junction of the British and Belgian lines north of Ypres ; the enemy might raid over the frozen canal. It was bitterly cold in the camps. There was much reconnoitring of the Elverdinghe defences and of the approaches thence to the front line.

On February 3rd the Battalion left " D " Camp and marched by Companies to the Cheese Market, Poperinghe, where it entrained at 5.50 for Bollezelle, arriving there at 10.15 p.m., and went into billets in the village. Here Battalion training was carried out so far as weather conditions would permit, but this training was often reduced to snow shovelling and even to snow balling ! On the 7th we returned to " O " Camp, and on the following day the Brigadier presented Military Medals to Company-Sergeant-Major Crichton, Sergeant White, and Lance-Corporals Pedder and Taylor. We were doing well in the football field hereabouts, and defeated the Welsh Regiment, the A.S.C., and the 8th Liverpools in succession.

On February 27th we moved up to Ypres again, but a thaw having set in made road transport and marching extremely difficult. When back in the line we moved over to the trenches in the Left Brigade Sector, and got to know Saint Jean, Wieltje and the trenches immediately north, including a dangerous spot north of Dixmude Gate, known as Well X-Roads. Headquarters were established at La Brique Post. On March 8th, 1917, Major P. E. Robathan, from a New Army Battalion of the Royal Welch Fusiliers, was posted to the Battalion and appointed second-in-command.   In the trenches a great deal of patrolling and investigation of the " Canadian Dugouts "—the old gun pits dating back to the First Battle of Ypres—which lay half-way between the lines.   Lieut. (afterwards Major) J. H. Evans was very active in this patrol work.   Trench life on the whole was uneventful, although enemy trench mortars were occasionally active.   After the transition period, October to December, 1916, the Battalion had shaken down and the new organization was working smoothly—new commanding officer, new second-in-command, and new adjutant.   Reinforcement officers had settled down, and the Battalion was gradually attaining the fine condition it enjoyed before the Third Battle of Ypres.

On April 16th we were relieved by the 10th Liverpool Scottish and proceeded to " Z " Camp. The following day the Battalion marched to Herzeele and went into billets, where a day or two was spent in cleaning up, organization, and bathing.   On the 22nd we marched to Buysscheure and stayed the night in billets.   The following day the Battalion reached its destination, Moulle, near St. Omer.   This pleasant region was all that could be desired.   The severe winter had given way to glorious spring, and feathered songsters, no less than ourselves, revelled in its advent.   The silence of the clear moonlight nights was varied by the song of the nightingale in almost embarrassing volume.

For some time the Quartermaster, Lieut. J. Crossley, had shown signs of the strain of the campaign, and on May 7th he returned to England for a rest, after two years at the front, and was relieved by Lieut. P. W. Powell.

CHAPTER VII.

THIRD BATTLE OF YPRES.

July 31st, 1917.

FROM April 23rd to May 6th we remained in Moulle under perfect conditions. The time was given over principally to practising the attack and consolidation of trenches. Training began early in the mornings and the afternoons were devoted to relaxation. The downs west of St. Omer formed ideal country for the re-conditioning of troops from the Salient, while by way of relaxation inter-Company league football matches were played. These were keenly contested and aroused close interest. St. Omer, too, lay within easy reach and a visit amply repaid the tedium of the brief journey. It was a sort of half-way house to Calais, and its amenities could not be excelled in another town of equal size. Its parks, even in wartime, were beautifully laid out and kept in irreproachable condition. The *beau monde* of St. Omer loved to dawdle in the gardens during these fine spring evenings, and an attractive wartime gaiety pervaded the whole town. Troops of various nationalities strolled about the boulevards or sat sipping coffee in the restaurants. Blue and khaki uniforms intermixed in the streets everywhere. Cadets wearing green bands were to be encountered at every corner. Flying Corps officers seemed to monopolise the club in the Grand Place. About the easy manners of the *boulevardier* there was an inexplicable charm, which, try as we might, we could never hope to imitate.

These pleasant days came to an end all too quickly, and on May 6th the Battalion began its return journey, marching to Buysscheure, where it went into billets for the night. The march was resumed the following morning to Arneke, where we entrained for Poperinghe and thence by march to " A " Camp, near Vlamertinghe, once more. Camp was shelled by long-range guns, causing some casualties.

On the evening of the 8th the Battalion relieved the 4th South Lancashire Regiment in the right sub-sector of the Potijze Sector, and started work immediately on the trenches and patrolling. During the night of the 11th the battalions on our left and right made raids on the enemy line, and we suffered a few casualties in consequence. During the night of the 13th our patrol of two officers and three other ranks encountered a strong enemy patrol of fifteen to twenty men and dispersed them. Life hereabouts alternated between the trenches in the Potijze Sector and billets in Ypres, and was of a more or less routine character. The Battalion played no part, save that of spectators, in the Second Army's capture of the Messines Ridge on June 7th. But before that operation lavish use of scaling ladders and shrapnel helmets was made in our trenches in order to deceive the enemy as to the front from which the expected attack would be delivered. At 3.10 a.m. on June 7th the Battalion saw to the south-east of Ypres nineteen gigantic poppies rise out of the darkness, the firing of the mines upon which the tunnelling companies had been occupied for two years; and even to-day the sight remains imprinted upon the visual memory.

On the evening of June 9th a smart little raid was carried out to ascertain if the Messines operations had resulted in any transfer of enemy troops from other areas. A party of thirty other ranks of the Battalion, under Second-Lieut. J. C. Alexander, entered the German lines at Ibex Trench, capturing six Germans and killing three others, with no casualties amongst our men. This was a most successful operation. Second-Lieut. J. Alexander was awarded the Military Cross for his leadership, while Lance-Corporal C. F. Cooper and Private J. McAlarney each received the Military Medal for bravery displayed during the raid.

On the morning of the 11th the Battalion marched to Poperinghe, entrained for Esquelbecq, and thence by route march to billets at Bollezeele for training.

On the 13th, after cleaning up and bathing parades, Companies were inspected by the Commanding Officer, Lieut.-Colonel G. B. Balfour.   On the 16th we moved by road to billets and bivouacs at Grand Difques (Headquarters and " B " Company) and Petite Difques (" A," " C " and " D " Companies), and Battalion training was resumed in the familiar downlands west of St. Omer.   The training was of a more advanced nature than in April, and included Brigade field-days with preparation for offensive warfare on a large scale. Training was generally completed by the early afternoon, so that many hours of sunshine remained to be enjoyed each day.

On June 30th Companies were inspected, and the transport moved by road to Wallon Cappel *en route* for the line once more, while on July 1st the Battalion marched to Lumbres and entrained for Brandhoek, relieving the 4th Liverpools at Derby Camp.   On our return to the forward area we found great activity everywhere : formation of dumps, preparation of gun positions, construction of tracks leading towards Ypres through the country between Vlamertinghe and Brielen.

On the 2nd we relieved the 6th Liverpools in the Wieltje right sub-sector of the line, and commenced work on trenches, sand-bagging and repairing wire. The usual patrols were sent out nightly.   There was increasing activity and unrest on both sides, and we received a heavy bombardment on the 3rd when the Brigade on our left carried out a raid.   On the 7th the Brigade on our right carried out a successful raid on the enemy trenches, and he retaliated with a gas-shell bombardment.   On July 9th we were relieved by the 4th Loyals and proceeded to billets at Derby Camp.

Nominally in billets, but truly in name only.   July 9th to 19th—a period of intense strain.   Companies lived in dugouts and strong points between Derby Camp and Ypres.   About 7 p.m. " A " Company (Captain R. Gardner, M.C.), like all the others, used to parade for a night's work in the trench area east of

Ypres—mostly carrying up materials and munitions from dumps at Potijze and St. Jean to selected positions for new dumps in the front line system—very trying, as Ypres and the forward area were shelled with gas the whole time and the parties had to work for long periods in box respirators. In the end the allotted tasks were all carried out, with heavyish casualties from shell fire and mustard-gas poisoning ; mustard gas began to be very bad from that point onwards. On getting through the gas area to the west of Ypres again the working parties not infrequently received salvoes of machine-gun fire from hostile aeroplanes a mile or so from their dugouts. Breakfast on return (5 to 6 a.m.) : sleep 6 a.m.—dinner (12 to 1 p.m.) : afternoon spent in administration and "paper" warfare with higher authority ; then back again to Ypres about 7 p.m. Ypres a grim sight : a mass of flames from burning dumps. Every evening until the 19th the Battalion paraded as strong as possible for work in the forward area. Intense activity was apparent everywhere, and there were visible signs that operations on a large scale were in early contemplation.

The objective of the Flanders offensive was the freeing of the north-west of Belgium. The attack was delayed, partly owing to the vastness of the preparations to be made on ground largely overlooked by the enemy, partly to the policy of associating the hardhit French with the work of freeing part of Belgium. Three armies were to be employed in the attack—the Second and Fifth British Armies and the First French Army. Refitting and organization proceeded apace, and on the morning of the 23rd Brigadier-General Stockwell addressed all Officers and N.C.O's regarding the forthcoming operations. On the 26th Companies were inspected and addressed by the Commanding Officer, Lieut.-Colonel G. B. Balfour, and on the evening of the 29th the Battalion, in fighting order with packs, proceeded to the concentration area.

We concentrated, under cover, in an assembly area just south of Vlamertinghe and were ordered to get as much rest as we could during the 30th. Some no doubt, slept as ordered, and others, like Julius Cæsar's troops before the battle with Ariovistus and his Germans in 58 B.C., began to think of making their wills.

In the early evening of the 30th the Battalion moved up by companies through the ruins and fires of Ypres towards Potijze and assembled in Congreve Walk, between Potijze Road and Lone Street, to wait for zero hour on the 31st.   Major P. E. Robathan was in command, Colonel Balfour, with other Officers, N.C.O.'s and men forming B. Echelon at the Transport. We had a long wait through the night while the first stage of the attack was carried out by the 165th and 166th Infantry Brigades.   At 3.30 a.m. on July 31st, under a barrage of more intense power than any previously recorded in the war, nine Divisions of the Fifth Army " went over the top," while attacks in co-operation were carried out on the right by the Second Army and on the left by the French.

By 9 a.m., after severe fighting, the assaulting battalions of the 165th and 166th Infantry Brigades had captured their objectives, known as the Blue Line and the Black Line, on the north side of the Ypres-Roulers railway, penetrating about one to one and a half miles from Wieltje into the German system. To the 164th Infantry Brigade fell the second stage of the attack, to pass through the 165th and 166th Infantry Brigades and capture the enemy's third line system, the Green Line or Gheluvelt-Langemarch Line, about one mile beyond the Black Line.

At 8.20 a.m. the 164th Infantry Brigade began its advance on a two-battalion frontage. The right front was formed by the 1/4th North Lancashire Regiment with the Battalion in support, and touch was to be kept on the right with battalions of the 45th Brigade (15th Division) ; the left front was formed by the 2/5th Lancashire Fusiliers supported by the 1/8th Liverpool (Irish). The slow advance from Congreve Walk towards the Black Line was carried out in its early stages according to schedule, and, in spite of a heavy retaliatory barrage, without

serious loss.   But before the Black Line was reached
it was found that the enemy still held some of his
concrete " pill boxes " (the term " farms " being a
courtesy title) and fighting became very severe, the
support battalions becoming involved.

But the advance from the Black Line to the Green
Line was the Battalion's real task.   Wonderful as the
barrage had been at the outset it lost a little in intensity
as the ranges lengthened and as time progressed.   The
Green Line was reached by all units of the Brigade and
was held for about three hours.   Among many who
fought with gallantry and devotion Lance-Sergeant
T. F. Mayson behaved with a distinction which won
him the Victoria Cross.   Single-handed he put out of
action two machine guns and their crews and during
the enemy counter-attack later in the day held up
the advance at an isolated post by Lewis Gun fire.

It was not possible to occupy the Green Line permanently (it was many weeks before British troops
again trod ground east of the Kansas Cross roads).
Although touch had been established on the Green
Line with the 15th Division on the right, the 39th
Division on the left had encountered such serious
difficulties that, although their right battalion gained
touch with the Lancashire Fusiliers on the Green
Line, a defensive flank had to be formed.

Moreover, in the early evening the enemy delivered
a most determined counter-attack against the Green
Line, and the Battalion, contesting, like the other
units, every inch of ground, was compelled to withdraw
to the Black Line, which it held against counter-
attack, and at 1.30 a.m. on August 1st received
orders to withdraw to the old British front line.
Battalion Headquarters moved from Pommern Redoubt, and about 5 a.m. reached the mined dugout
in Oxford Trench, where they joined Lieut.-Colonel
Hindle, D.S.O., of the 4th Loyals, and his battalion
headquarters.

The remnants of the Battalion and those of the 4th
Loyals, manned the old front line from the top of
New John Street to Warwick Farm.   It was not until

midday that all the survivors were collected—about 150 in all. Lieut. C. E. Withey took command of the front line, having under him Second-Lieuts. Lauder, Newbold, Gribble, Latham and Ellwood, and Second-Lieut. Lonsdale, of the 4th Loyals. Information was received that the enemy had driven back our advanced posts upon the Frezenberg Line and was preparing to assault that line. Preparations were accordingly made to hold the old front line as strongly as possible and a defence was quickly organised.

Heavy rain had rendered the old trench almost untenable, and the task of reforming trench duties and taking round the rations was extremely difficult. Towards midnight fifty stragglers were brought up from Transport lines, under Second-Lieut. Lingford, to reinforce the garrison. No casualties were sustained in the fire trench, although it was intermittently shelled. On August 2nd information was received that the Brigade was to be relieved by the 108th Brigade. The relieving troops arrived at 1.30 p.m., and relief was reported complete by 2.30. The situation was quiet during the morning, and no further casualties were sustained.

Upon relief by the 9th Royal Irish Rifles, Companies moved off independently, and by 5 p.m. had all reached the old concentration area at Vlamertinghe. Battalion Headquarters boarded a motor lorry outside St. Jean and had not proceeded very far when a heavy shell exploded just behind. Three were seriously wounded (two of whom afterwards died) and two slightly wounded. Colonel Hindle, of the 4th Loyals, Major Robathan, and the other occupants of the wagon had very narrow escapes. On reaching the concentration area everyone received a welcome rum ration— an indulgence which in a few instances produced curious effects ! Food was ready and also baths and clean clothes. Colonel Balfour and the Officers and N.C.O.'s of the " B " List were assiduous in their attentions to the survivors. They had had information of the progress of the battle from wounded Officers passing through the Clearing Station at Vlamertinghe

Mill. At 8.45 the Battalion left the concentration area and proceeded by buses—in a long convoy with the other units of the Brigade—to the Watou No. 3 Area, *via* Brandhoek and Poperinghe.

Camp outside Watou was reached about 1 a.m. on the 3rd, rations and transport arriving a little later. Heavy rain had fallen and the camp was a quagmire, but the exhausted troops threw themselves down thankfully and were soon oblivious to their discomforts. Little else, except sleep, was done during the day, but stock was taken of the situation and casualties were estimated. The Battalion sustained the following Officer casualties :—

Capt. W. R. Pattinson ... Wounded.
Capt. H. A. Brocklebank ... Wounded and missing.
Second-Lieut. G. W. Ford ... Killed.
Second-Lieut. J. A. McGill... Wounded.
Second-Lieut. H. J. Warbrick Wounded.
Second-Lieut. J. C. Alexander,
   M.C. ... ... Wounded.
Second-Lieut. F. C. Gilling ... Wounded.
Lieut. S. F. Walker ... ... Wounded.
Second-Lieut. J. D. Johnstone Killed.
Second-Lieut. R. Bradley ... Killed.
Second-Lieut. J. R. Gaulter Wounded.
Second-Lieut. T. H. Middle-
   ton ... ... Wounded.
Second-Lieut. P. C. Taylor ... Wounded.

Other ranks : 21 killed, 145 wounded and 46 missing. The Battalion captured four machine guns and its fair share of the 500 prisoners captured by the Division. The casualties of the Battalion were not so serious as those of other units in the Brigade. This grievous toll was the price paid for an operation in which the Battalion again vindicated its reputation for valour and devotion to duty. That this view was shared by the higher authorities is shown by the following communications, which it is fitting should be given here in full :—

55TH (WEST LANCASHIRE) DIVISION.
SPECIAL ORDER OF THE DAY.
3rd August, 1917.

To all Ranks of the 55th (West Lancashire) Division.

Before you went into action on the 31st July, I told you how confident I was that the Division would do its duty, and maintain its reputation, and the reputations of the grand Regiments to which you belong.

You have done more than that.

The attack you made on the 31st is worthy to rank with the great deeds of the British Army in the past, and has added fresh glory to the record of that Army.

The courage, determination, and self-sacrifice shown by Officers, Warrant Officers, Non Commissioned Officers and men is beyond praise. It is a fine exhibition of true discipline, which comes from the mutual confidence of all ranks in themselves, their comrades, their leaders and those under them. This in its turn is the product of hard training. Your doings on the 31st show how well you have turned this training to account.

You have captured every inch of the objectives allotted to you. It was not your fault that you could not hold all you took. You have broken and now hold in spite of weather and counter attacks, a line that the enemy has strengthened and consolidated at his leisure for more than two years.

· This will, I believe, be the beginning of the end. When your turn comes to go forward again you will know your own strength—and the enemy will know it too.

I am proud of what you have done, and am confident that with such troops ultimate victory is certain.

(Signed)   H. S. JEUDWINE,
Major General,
Commanding 55th (West Lancashire) Division.

FIFTH ARMY,
G.A. 790/7.
3rd August, 1917.

XIX CORPS.

The Army Commander wishes to convey his thanks and congratulations to the G.O.C. and all Ranks of the 164th Brigade on their fine performance on July 31st. They carried out their task in a most gallant manner, and fought splendidly to retain their hold on the ground won.

All Officers showed energy, courage and initiative in dealing with the situation, and the men under their command, in spite of heavy losses, did their utmost by carrying out their orders, to ensure our success and the enemy's defeat.

Great credit and praise is due to the G.O.C., 164th Brigade, for the magnificent behaviour of the troops under his command.

(Signed)   N. MALCOLM,
Major General, G.S.

2.

164TH INFANTRY BRIGADE,
No. G. 280.

1/4TH ROYAL LANCS. REGT.

The Brigadier General Commanding has much pleasure in forwarding the above remarks of the Army Commander, and directs that these be communicated to all ranks.

He considers that all credit and praise is due to the Officers and men of the Brigade.

(Signed)   G. SURTEES, *2nd Lieut.,*
for Captain,
Acting Brigade Major, 164th Infantry Brigade.
6th August, 1917.

The process of " cleaning up " and re-equipment was begun. All Companies attended baths. Narratives were written by Company Commanders, Platoon Commanders and Section Leaders. From these a Battalion Report was compiled by Major Robathan and submitted to Brigade. Rain fell persistently throughout the day but the evening was fine. At 2-30 a.m. on the 5th August orders were received from Brigade for a move to an area on the Lines of Communication, and at 7-30 a.m. the Battalion left camp and proceeded to Abeele Station, where it halted for an hour until the time for entrainment arrived. This was completed by 11 a.m., and travelling via the Hazebrouck switch line and St. Omer the Battalion detrained at Audruicq, and was conveyed in motor lorries down the valley of the Hem, via Nordausques and Tournehem, to Bonningues-les-Ardres. Here excellent and commodious billets had been arranged for both Officers and men. The village had not been occupied by troops for some time, and the inhabitants gave the Battalion a splendid welcome. The well-wooded valley and surrounding moors were a delightful change from the flats of Flanders. With us in the same village were billeted the 8th Liverpools, while Brigade Headquarters were at Tournehem.

Reorganization of Companies was commenced. " A " Company under Lieut. Withey, " B " Company under 2nd Lieut- Evans, " C " Company under Capt. Procter, and " D " Company under 2nd Lieut. R. M. Senton. Reinforcements were arriving and were posted to the different Companies. On parade the Commanding Officer addressed the Battalion, expressing his pride in what they had done. A long and pleasant period ensued in these delighful surroundings, the time being devoted to training in the morning and to recreation in the afternoon and evening. A Sports' Committee was formed and the utmost keenness was displayed in the various competitions. A Battalion Sports and Gymkhana was held on the afternoon of the 16th August, from 2 to 9 p.m. This was favoured by splendid weather, and there was a large gathering of interested spectators. There was a keen struggle for the Inter-Company Cup offered for competition by the Commanding Officer, this being eventually won on the following day, when the sports were continued, by the Transport. These wound up in the evening with a Battalion Concert, organized by 2nd Lieut. Mudie, a gifted entertainer, who himself contributed his little masterpiece " Three Hundred and Sixty-five Days." A delightful addition to these light-hearted proceedings took place when orders were received from Brigade for forty-eight hours' leave to be granted to Officers to visit the coast of France, and twenty-four hours' leave to other Ranks to visit Calais. In the Brigade Sports, Battalion representatives were uniformly successful, the Tug-of-War, 2 Miles, 1 Mile, and Association Football falling to us.

Reinforcements continued to arrive, amongst them being Second-Lieuts. E. D. Howard, Veevers, White, E. Haslam, N. Whittaker, T. H. Pritchard, and R. G. Hatcher.

Training went on apace, and distinction was conferred on the Battalion when a Platoon, under 2nd Lieut. Ellwood, was selected to give a demonstration attack upon a strong point. Officers and N.C.O.'s from Divisions in the Fifth Army attended this demonstration, which went on for some days, and on 19th August, Field Marshal Sir Douglas Haig visited the Division and saw the Battalion at work in field operations.

During our stay at Bonningues-les-Ardres, Lieut.-Col. G. B. Balfour was invalided from the Battalion with scarlet fever, and command was taken by Major P. E. Robathan. Captain and Adjutant J. Way returned to England for a period of home service, and was succeeded as Adjutant by Capt. R. Gardner. On the 6th September we marched to Moulle, of old acquaintance, and fired field practices by Companies, but preparation soon began for a return to the Ypres Salient. During the Division's period of absence from the line, several attempts by other Divisions had been made to advance from the Black Line, but without marked success. On the 10th the Battalion, together with the remainder of the Brigade, took part in Divisional operations on ground representing the area the Division will operate on in the forthcoming attack.

On the 14th the Battalion moved by road to Audruicq, and there entrained for Ypres, where we were billeted in tent and bivouacs near Goldfish Chateau. On the following day a hostile squadron of aeroplanes dropped three bombs on the camp, killing one and wounding three others of other regiments. Capt. Wilson, our Medical Officer, was also slightly wounded, but remained on duty. Next morning the camp was again bombed by enemy aircraft, this time killing three and wounding five other ranks of the Battalion. Bombs dropped a few yards from the tent used as the Battalion Orderly Room, the Battalion Runners and Headquarters details were the sufferers. Later in the day Second-Lieut. Whittaker was wounded in the arm by an anti-aircraft machine gun bullet.

On the 17th the Battalion was finally organized and, after the news of Sergt. Mayson's V.C. had come through, in the evening marched through St. Jean and Wieltje to the Concentration Area, " B " and " D " Companies Headquarters in Call Reserve (old German Reserve trench), and " C " and " A " in the old British front line. We incurred casualties in 3 killed and 4 wounded. The following day Officers and N.C.O.'s reconnoitred the front line and position of attack, and " D " Company relieved the 10th Liverpool Scottish in the front shell-hole system, the Battalion suffering 3 killed and 7 wounded in these operations. On the 19th September we were fitted out with stores and extra rations, and moved to positions of attack in shell holes between Somme and Hinducutt, with Headquarters at Capricorn Keep.

Major P. E. Robathan commanded the Battalion, with Captain J. H. Evans as Second-in-command. The 164th Infantry Brigade attacked on a two-battalion frontage, 1/4th Royal Lancashire Regiment on the right, 2/5th Lancashire Fusiliers on the left. 1/4th North Lancashire Regiment acted as support to the Battalion, and 1/5th Royal Lancashire Regiment, from 166th Infantry Brigade, was a reserve Battalion placed under the command of the Brigadier General Commanding, 164th Infantry Brigade. The Battalion had orders to reach an intermediate objective, the dotted Red Line; 1/4th North Lancashire Regiment, after supporting the Battalion at the outset, was to pass through it and advance to the Green Line. The attack was on a vast scale, eleven Divisions being employed.

During the night of the 19th-20th September platoons took up their positions in shell holes west of the line Somme—Hinducott amidst a severe bombardment, which had been going on for some days. At zero hour (5-40 a.m. on the 20th September) the first wave advanced on the enemy positions between Hinducott and Somme, and reached its first objective in spite of stubborn opposition, especially from Aisne Farm and Loos. Here, after a slight pause in the barrage, " A " and " C " Companies continued to advance, but sustained heavy casualties from enfilade fire. Owing to appalling mud, and determined opposition from the garrisons of "pill-boxes," the advance was slow, and the support Battalion, 1/4th North Lancashire Regiment, soon became involved in the fighting. The Battalion reached the dotted Red Line, but the support Battalion was not sufficiently strong to continue the advance, and eventually both Battalions held a line from Schuler Galleries to Loos, under heavy bombardment and enfilade fire from both flanks. Capt. A. P. Procter, commanding " C " Company, was placed in command of the front line, which was manned by both Battalions and reinforcements from the reserve Battalion, 1/5th Royal Lancashire Regiment.

Patrols were sent out during the night to ascertain the enemy's positions, and forward posts pushed ahead. During the morning of the 21st, small parties of the enemy were observed coming down the forward slopes in front of Gravenstafel carrying Red Cross flags.   At 4-50 p.m. the 8th Liverpool (Irish) occupied Schuler Farm and pushed forward to the Green Line, at the same time the 5th Lancashire Fusiliers moved forward from Schuler Galleries towards Cross Cotts.   In the evening the enemy intensely bombarded our front line, but no counter attack was made.   During the night posts were pushed forward to prepare for a further advance next night.   At dawn on the 22nd, the enemy heavily shelled our front line, and a small party was seen advancing towards us. Our artillery and machine guns replied, and the hostile bombardment ceased.   During the morning our front line was again heavily shelled by the enemy, and also again in the evening, but no attack was made against us.   Just before dawn on the 23rd, our front line was intensely bombarded, our machine guns replying, and the bombardment died down.   On the afternoon of the 23rd, preparations were made for the relief of the 39th Division.   Guides had assembled at Battalion Headquarters, Capricorn Keep, and were about to lead to their positions the guides of the incoming unit, when, at 5-15 p.m., the whole of the Battalion area was subjected to a violent bombardment, which lasted till 8 p.m.   Practically no casualties were sustained.   What it must have been like for the Companies out in the open can only be imagined, but in the Battalion Headquarters' dugout, with entrance conveniently facing the enemy, the occupants waited, with what philosophy they could, for a shell to intrude and sever their connection with the Third Battle of Ypres.   But none came.   After some excitement concerning the whereabouts of a platoon, the Battalion was relieved at 1-45 a.m. on September 24th by two platoons of the 2/6th North Staffordshire Regiment The survivors tramped through Wieltje to St. Jean for the last time, and said farewell to Ypres.   From Vlamertinghe we went by train and bus to Watou.

During these operations the Battalion sustained the following casualties :—

Captain C. E. Withey and Second-Lieut. E. T. White killed.   Second-Lieuts. G. C. Lingford (died of wounds),

G. A. Taylor, T. H. Pritchard, C. H. Newbold, R. M. Senton, and J. Thompson, wounded, and R. G. Hatcher, died of wounds. Second-Lieut. C. G. Howard missing.

Other Ranks: Killed, 37; Wounded, 155; Wounded and Missing, 1; Shell Shock, 6; Missing, 24. Total, all ranks, 233. At a later date the Officer temporarily in Command, Major P. E. Robathan, also went to hospital suffering from the effects of gas.

The conspicuous value and success of these strenuous operations is amply testified by the following communications received from the higher authorities :—

55TH (WEST LANCASHIRE) DIVISION.
ORDER OF THE DAY.

1. The following telegrams have been received :—

" Fifth Army wire begins. The Army Commander wishes to thank all arms and all ranks for their splendid efforts in to-day's battle. Co-operation between Infantry, Artillery and Flying Corps has been excellent, and very important successes have been gained all along the front. Ends."

" Corps Commander thanks Field and Heavy Artillery for their good work, and the Forward Observation Officers for the very useful and timely information sent in. Ends."

" Corps Commander congratulates 9th and 55th Divisions and thanks them for their success to-day. Ends."

2. The Major-General Commanding wishes to add his thanks and congratulations to all arms and ranks of the Division.

There is no doubt whatever that in addition to making a very substantial advance over difficult ground, stubbornly defended, well organized, and liberally provided with strong cover, artillery and machine guns, the Division, aided most ably by the Corps Heavy Artillery, succeeded in dealing the enemy a very heavy blow, and causing him severe losses.

G

Success was due to the fine determination shown by all ranks and the hearty co-operation of Artillery, Engineers, Infantry, Machine Gun Companies, Trench Mortars and the R.A.M.C. with each other, which is the sign of a united and disciplined Division.

(Signed) T. ROSE PRICE,

Lieut.-Colonel,

General Staff, 55th Division.

21st September, 1917.

55TH (WEST LANCASHIRE) DIVISION.
ORDER OF THE DAY.

The following telegrams from the V Corps have been received :—

" The Commander-in-Chief visited Corps Headquarters this evening and expressed himself very pleased in the work of both Divisions and sends them his congratulations and thanks."

" Fifth Army wire begins. Please congratulate 55th Division on the gallant defence of Hill 37 yesterday, and upon the energy and resource displayed by Commanders on the spot in organizing counter attacks. Ends."

(Signed) T. ROSE PRICE,

Lieut.-Colonel,

General Staff, 55th Division.

23rd September, 1917.

55TH (WEST LANCASHIRE) DIVISION.
ORDER OF THE DAY.

The following telegram has been received from the Right Honourable E. G. V. Earl of Derby, K.G., G.C.V.O., C.B., Secretary of State for War :—

" General Jeudwine, 55th Division Headquarters, B.E.F.

" Well done 55th West Lancashire Division. Accept my most hearty congratulations. I sincerely trust your losses are not heavy.

Derby."

(Signed)   T. ROSE PRICE,
Lieut.-Colonel,
General Staff, 55*th Division*.

24th September, 1917.

55TH (WEST LANCASHIRE) DIVISION.

ORDER OF THE DAY.

The following telegram has been received from Fifth Army :—

" 55TH DIVISION.

" Please convey to all ranks 55th Division the Army Commander's congratulations on the fine record of the Division during the hard fighting of the past two months. The Army Commander wishes specially to thank all ranks for their splendid efforts, which have contributed greatly to the success of the last attack, and to wish them all good luck and success in the future. Despite their long period in the line prior to commencement of operations they have well maintained and increased their high reputation.

" FIFTH ARMY."

The following telegram has been received from the West Lancashire Reserve Brigade :—

" G.O.C. 55TH DIVISION, FRANCE.

" Brigadier General Stuart and all ranks West Lancashire Reserve Brigade send heartiest congratulations to West Lancashire Division on their splendid success."

(Signed)   T. ROSE PRICE,
Lieut.-Colonel,
General Staff, 55*th Division*.

27th September, 1917.

While it is true that virtue is its own reward, and kindles a pure unquenchable flame in men's hearts, it would be idle to deny that these cordial messages of appreciation of their sacrifices cheered the Battalion profoundly and steeled their determination for further efforts in the stern task yet to be accomplished.

On the 25th we spent a day cleaning up and resting. At 1 p.m. Major Robathan addressed all Officers and other ranks who had been in battle. Reinforcements as follows were received during the day: Second-Lieuts. L. R. Keighley, J. R. Rundle, H. Walkden, A. J. Thorpe, F. J. Shuker, R. L. Purnell, B. H. Gough, and 18 other Ranks. At 9.30 p.m. we moved by march route to Hopoutre Station and entrained for Bapaume West, in the Lens area. We arrived here at 12.30 p.m. on the 26th, and then marched via Bapaume—Le Transloy—Rocquigny and Bus, to Ytres (not to be confused with Ypres) to a camp at Vallulart Wood. This was a long and tiring march; 15 men dropped out, but every one of these rejoined. Here Platoon and Company training of an easy nature was carried out until the 2nd October, when the Battalion was again on the move. At 9.15 a.m., accompanied by the Band and Transport, we marched out of camp and proceeding via Etricourt—where we marched past the G.O.C. 55th Division—Manancourt—where the Brigadier General Commanding 164th Brigade watched the Battalion marching—Nurlu—Aizecourt-le-Bas to Longavesnes where we arrived in billets at 12.50 p.m. The weather set in cold and wet and was a disagreeable change from the perfect conditions we had enjoyed for several weeks. Captain A. P. Procter was temporarily in command of the Battalion.

Platoon and Company training was resumed and routes to the new trench sector at St. Emilie were reconnoitred. A rousing Rugby football match was played between the Battalion and Flying Corps Squadron XV. " The " Aces " were too good for the " King's Own," and we went under by 13 points to 5. Major Robathan rejoined from hospital, together with 12 Officer reinforcements. On the 12th October we marched into Brigade Reserve at St. Emilie, under wet and unpleasant conditions, relieving the 6th King's Liverpools, while on the following evening the Battalion took over trenches from the 7th King's Liverpool Regiment in the right sub-sector of the Right Sector at St. Emilie. Dispositions were as follows : Right front line Cat Post " C " Company. Left front line Gillemont Farm, " A " Company, Support Company, Duncan and Doleful Posts, " B " Company. Reserve Company " D " Company and Battalion Headquarters at Ken Lane. At 9.50 p.m. the relief was completed with no casualties. We found the trenches in very fair condition, but much draining, reveting and duck-boarding required.

A comparatively quiet period followed. There were occasional heavy bombardments by the enemy's Minenwerfers and Granatenwerfers. These did con-siderable damage to our trenches but no casualties occurred, and our Trench Mortars replied vigorously. Trench life alternated with periods in Brigade Support in St. Emilie and Lempire, until the Battalion went into Divisional Reserve on 2nd November in Longa-vesnes. The following Officer reinforcements joined during October : Second-Lieuts. R. Smith, R. W. Higginson, W. M. Stewart, G. Field, R. S. Dane, J. Mackay, G. F. Raeside, A. J. Dartnell, G. N. Russell, A. H. Pemberton, W. McAndrew, J. H. Sykes, N. Smith, C. J. Holland, G. W. Ferguson. Corpl. W. Masters, " D " Company, was killed in action, and Lance Corpl. A. Clark, " D " Company, Pte. H. Bolton, " B " Company and Pte. H. Caton, " D " Company, wounded, the two latter accidentally. The following Decorations were awarded to Officers, N.C.O.s and men for gallantry and devotion to duty in the fighting of September 20th/23rd :—

Military Cross.—A/Capt. A. P. Procter, Lieut. and Qr.-Mr. P. W. Powell, Second-Lieuts. A. S. Latham and G. A. Taylor.

Distinguished Conduct Medal.—C.S.M. D. Graham, Sergt. F. S. Yates, Sergt. A. Burton, Lance-Sergt. J. R. Pearson.

Military Medal.—Corpl. T. Wright, Pte. A. E. Ashburn, Corpl. E. Lockey, Lance-Sergt. W. Whiteside, C.Q.M. Sergt. W. G. Hinds, Pte. J. Wild, Sergt. H. Myers, Lance-Corpl. H. Dobbs, Lance-Corpl. T. Chester and Pte. E. G. Robinson.

Lieut.-Colonel G. B. Balfour then returned from sick leave to command the Battalion.

The period in Longavesnes was spent in Company training and organized games. Medals were presented to the winners of the Football Competition, and the Cup offered by Colonel Balfour was presented to the Transport for the Sports held at Bonningues in September. The Battalion was also exercised in the Practice Attack as a preliminary to the real operations now impending. The Battalion Band, under Band Sergt. Rickwood, had at this time attained to a fine standard of efficiency, and, while adding considerably to the amenities, were a real asset on the march. At 5 p.m. on the 17th November we marched out from Longavesnes en route for St. Emilie, a distance of 6 miles, and reached billets at 6.45 p.m. At 7 p.m. on the 19th the Battalion marched out by Companies at half-hour intervals to take up attack positions in the right sub-sector of the Right Sector. (Gillemont Farm.)

At 2.45 a.m. on the 20th November, Companies were all in position for the attack. Their disposition was " A " Company and 1 Platoon " D " Company on the right in Stokes Trench. " B " Company and 1 Platoon " D " Company in centre in Stokes Trench. " C " Company and 1 Platoon " D " Company on left in Blunt Nose. One Company 4th Loyal North Lancashire Regiment held Cat Post—Dog Trench during the attack. At zero hour, 6.20 a.m., the attack pushed forward under a heavy barrage of guns, trench mortars and machine guns. The enemy wire was found to be very thick and generally unbroken, and his barrage was quickly put down on our front line and approaches. This barrage increased as time went on ; guns from both flanks evidently being brought into action. The Right Flank made good progress in spite of strong opposition, and all but gained their final objective. The Centre Company from the start encountered heavy machine gun fire, and when they reached the enemy immediate support line, were met with showers of bombs and rifle grenades, the enemy making a very stubborn resistance.

They pushed on, however, and made progress for a time, but being greatly outnumbered, and suffering heavy casualties, they were held up short of the final objective. The Left Company encountered almost uncut wire, but, forcing their way through, they pushed on until, running short of bombs, and meeting superior forces of the enemy, they were held up.

The Left Company were gradually forced back, as the attack on the left Battalion had failed, while the Centre Company were ejected from their forward position, and were hard pressed to hold their own. Towards noon the Left Company had been forced back to the enemy front line, while the Centre Company were in danger of being cut off from the Right Company, who were themselves being forced gradually back.

At 12.45 p.m. reinforcements were sent up from the 5th King's Liverpools, and, with the help of these 2 Platoons, the Centre Company attempted to consolidate the enemy front line, and join up with the Right Company. About 1 p.m. the enemy made a very determined attack, and forced the Centre Company back into our original line by weight of numbers, and superiority of bombs, rifle grenades, etc. Enemy trench mortars and artillery were active on our Support Line and roads of approach. The Right Company, finding both flanks in the air, and being attacked by superior numbers, fell back to avoid being surrounded and cut off altogether. The fighting all morning was particularly fierce, but the enemy were superior in numbers and ammunition, and great difficulty was experienced in getting ammunition through the enemy barrage to the attacking Companies. The Companies reorganized in our front line, and devoted all their efforts to clearing the trenches of wounded, debris, etc.

The Battalion was relieved during the night of the 20th/21st by the 4th Loyals, and moved into dugouts in Ken Lane—Sart Lane, the relief being completed by 4.30 a.m. The day was spent resting, cleaning clothes, arms, etc., and salving of equipment, arms, and the removal of dead from the front line. At 6 p.m. on the 22nd Companies moved off independently and concentrated at St. Emilie, where they were met by the Band, and marched to billets in Longavesnes, and became part of the Divisional Reserve. At 2.30 p.m. on the 23rd the Major-General Commanding the Division came and spoke to the Battalion, which paraded in fatigue dress. In the course of his remarks, the General stated that " Although the Battalion did not hold their gains, yet they more than achieved the object of this attack. A considerable quantity of men and guns were kept employed opposite our front, and so assisted our advance at Cambrai. No enemy reinforcements left our front until late in the day."

The following casualties were sustained during this attack :—

Officers.—Killed, Lieut. A. M. Clark (displayed splendid leadership in Gillemont Crescent), Second-Lieut. A. J. Dartnell. Wounded, Second-Lieut. J. R. Rundle (died of wounds), Capt. T. R. Blain, Second-Lieuts. R. Smith, J. Mackay, J. H. Sykes, G. Field, L. R. Keighley. Total, 9.

Other Ranks.—Killed 9, Wounded 113, Missing 80. Total 202.

There was little repose in this period of " rest " and the general atmosphere was one of tension. On the 29th the Battalion was ordered to " Stand To " and be ready to move immediately, as heavy enemy attacks were expected opposite the Divisional front. At 8.30 a.m. on the 30th we moved off by Companies to concentrate with the rest of the 164th Brigade near St. Emilie. At 10.30 a.m. the Battalion was ordered to move to Epehy and hold on at all costs.

The enemy had broken through on the flank of the Left Brigade, and cut off almost the whole of the Brigade in the line. At 12 noon Companies extended to N.E. of Epehy and advanced in extended order to reinforce the 5th King's Own, who were being forced back from their forward positions. Companies dug in a new line about 300 yards behind the front line held by the 5th King's Own. The enemy were held, and we commenced to consolidate the position. The evening was fairly quiet and our casualties had been small.

On the 1st December the Battalion were in immediate support to the remains of the 166th Brigade, on the left of the Divisional front. The line held was as follows : From Fallen Tree Road on the right to Fourteen Willows Road and thence to Epehy—Villers Guislain Road on the left. During the early morning a party of the 5th King's Own and 10th Liverpool Scottish, who had been surrounded in Limerick Post for nearly twenty-four hours, fought their way out and regained our lines. This party reinforced the front line and enabled closer touch to be gained with the 5th Lancashire Fusiliers on our left. At 6 a.m. an attack was due to commence by Tanks and Cavalry, with the intention of re-taking Villers Guislain, but no action was observed, although the artillery activity on the left increased considerably. At 9 a.m. however an attack by cavalry commenced. Two Squadrons advanced along the Epehy—Villers Guislain road and attempted to attack in the direction of Villers Guislain, but they were so badly cut up by artillery fire and Machine Guns that they withdrew to Epehy. Cavalry also attacked from Little Priel Farm on the right, and managed to make progress. One Squadron attempted to approach Villers Guislain by pushing along the valley from Little Priel Farm, but were met with heavy machine gun fire from Parr's Bank, and although they held on to a forward position near Fourteen Willows Road for some time, they suffered heavy casualties, and were ultimately forced to withdraw.

The enemy made no further attempt to attack the Brigade front, devoting his efforts to consolidating the ground gained, but his artillery, Machine Guns and snipers were very active all morning. At 1 p.m. we launched a counter attack with the intention of retaking Meath, Kildare and Limerick Posts, and making these posts a line of resistance. About 200 of the 5th King's Own, 10th Liverpool Scottish and 5th Loyals, together with 2 Squadrons of Indian Cavalry, constituted the attacking force. Inadequate Artillery support, and heavy enemy Machine Gun fire were mainly responsible for the failure of the attack, and the survivors returned to our front line, having suffered severely. During the attack " A " Company moved up from immediate support to the front line, S. of Fourteen Willows Road.

At 4.30 p.m. enemy Artillery became very active, Battalion Headquarters in Fourteen Willows Road, our front line and support line to the right of the Epehy—Villers Guislain Road, were heavily shelled for about half an hour. As evening drew near, however, conditions became normal. The 8th Liverpool Irish advanced on the left of Epehy—Villers Guislain Road in support of the 4th Loyals, and eventually gained touch with the left flank of the 166th Brigade on the right of Epehy—Villers Guislain Road. The 166th Infantry Brigade, including the 4th King's Own, were relieved during the night by the 110th Infantry Brigade, 21st Division, and went into billets in St. Emilie, the relief being completed at 1.30 a.m. on the 2nd December, and all Companies had arrived in billets by 3.30 a.m. The day was spent in resting and cleaning equipment and clothes, but we were again under orders to be ready to move at half an hour's notice. Reserves of ammunition, grenades, tools and rations were brought up to establishment.

At 4 p.m. on the 4th December orders were received for the Battalion to move up to Sandbag Alley to reinforce the Reserves of the 165th Brigade. Companies moved off independently and all were safely in dugouts by 8 p.m. In anticipation of an imminent enemy attack we " stood to," " C " and " D " Companies manning Queen's Trench, and " A " and " B " Companies remaining in Sandbag Alley. All being quiet on the Brigade front Companies stood down at 7.30 a.m. At midnight on the 5th the 165th Brigade including the 4th King's Own, were relieved by the 48th Infantry Brigade, 16th Division. On completion Companies marched independently to St. Emilie. Accommodation was exceedingly scarce, and the whole Battalion were crowded into one Adrian Hut. The weather was very cold, dry and frosty. At 5.30 a.m. on the 6th we were called on to man the Brown Line as Reserves to the 48th Infantry Brigade, in case of attack. After considerable difficulty this was completed, but the morning proved exceptionally quiet, and the Battalion was ordered by Division to return to billets in St. Emilie.

At 1 p.m. verbal orders were received from Colonel Eden, A.A. and Q.M.G., that the Battalion would be relieved that day, and were to proceed to Longavesnes. Accordingly at 2 p.m. we marched to the Transport Lines at Villers Faucon and had tea. At 5 p.m., accompanied by the Band, the Battalion marched into Longavesnes, and proceeded thence by bus to Peronne, which was reached at 7.15, and by 8 p.m. the whole Battalion had reached the Camp. The whole of the 7th was spent in resting and making preparations for continuing the move. The weather turned wet in the evening. At 10 a.m. on the 8th following the 8th Liverpool Irish and 5th Lancashire Fusiliers, we marched to Peronne-Flamicourt Station and entrained, leaving at 12 noon for Beaumetz-les-Loges. On arrival at 9.30 p.m. we formed up behind the 8th Liverpool Irish and marched into billets at Lattre St. Quentin at 2 a.m. on the 9th after a tiring march in the rain. The route travelled was via Simoncourt —Wanquentin—Hauteville—Lattre St. Quentin. The remainder of the day was spent in resting and cleaning up, rain falling almost the whole day. The Transport, which had marched all the way from

Peronne, halting for the night of the 8th/9th at Courcelles, arriving at 6 p.m.

On the 10th at 9 a.m. the Battalion was again on the march, moving via Avesnes le Comte—Manin —Givenchy le Noble—Penin—Tinques, arriving in billets in Bailleul-aux-Cornailles at 2 p.m., the weather being fine but cold.   The following day at 10-30 a.m. the march was resumed via Monchy—Breton (where we marched past the Brigadier General Commanding 164th Infantry Brigade)—La Thieuloye—Valhuon Hestrus to Eps, where billets were reached at 3 p.m., the weather being fine.   On the 12th at 10 a.m. the Battalion marched to Crepy via Petit Anvin, billets being reached at 12 noon.   At 10.30 a.m. on the 13th, we made what was to be the last of this series of marches moving via Fruges—Monteville—Radhinghem—Wandonne and Dennebroccq to Reclinghem where we arrived in billets at 3.25 p.m.   The weather continued warm and bright.

After the hard fighting and strenuous exercises of the past few months, the long period of rest in Reclinghem which followed was not unacceptable. Freed from trench worries for the time being, leisurely but thorough attention could be paid to reorganization, platoon and company training, and this was the general routine now followed.   The Brigade Baths at Coyecque also received a full measure of patronage.   The weather turned cold, with leaden skies threatening snow, and this duly arrived to give a traditional setting to Christmas Day.   This was our third Christmas in France and Belgium, and as the previous two had been spent in the trenches at Authuille and Ypres respectively, special efforts were made on this occasion to mark this genial festival in a more fitting manner.   A very pleasant day was spent, and one that lingers in the memory.   There was a Voluntary Church Parade in the morning, which took place in the School at Reclinghem, and at 3.30 p.m. the Brigadier General Commanding, accompanied by the Commanding Officer, visited all the Companies in turn at dinner.   The Sergeants, after attending to the men's needs, had their dinner at 5.30 p.m., and they also received a visit from the Commanding Officer, when the usual compliments of the season were exchanged. All Officers dined together in the Headquarters Mess at 7.30 p.m., when the Battalion Band was in attendance, and rendered an appropriate programme in a pleasing manner. Altogether a memorable day.

New Year's Day, 1918, was observed, by order of the Brigadier, as a holiday from all parades, except for short inspection parades in the morning. Sports were indulged in during the day, but the weather conditions were too severe to admit of organized games. News was received that the Brigadier General Commanding (General Stockwell) had been awarded the C.M.G., and a congratulatory message was sent from the Colonel and all Officers. In spite of the adverse weather, which necessitated much clearing of snow, training was persevered with, and on the 19th January the First Army Commander, General Sir H. S. Horne, inspected the 164th Infantry Brigade Group on the parade ground of the 5th Lancashire Fusiliers, at Coyecque. He took the opportunity of presenting medal ribands awarded to various members of the Battalion, Officers, N.C.O.s and men. The massed Brigade Buglers, under Corporal Parry of the 4th King's Own, sounded the General Salute. The Battalion Band played during the Inspection, and, as the various units marched past, played the " March Past " of each Unit. The Army Commander, in his address, referred to the fight at Gueudecourt on September 27th, 1916, on which occasion the 164th Brigade was last under his Command—as Commander of the XIV Corps. He complimented the Brigade on its fine turnout, and steadiness on parade.

CHAPTER VIII.

GIVENCHY.

TIME was passing, the enemy unconquered, and our pleasant stay in Reclinghem came to an end. Companies engaged in preparations for the Battalion move towards the Line. At 8.15 a.m. on the 7th February we proceeded by march route via Beaumetz-les-Aire, Laires, Febvin, Palfart to Ligny-les-Aires, where billets were reached at 12.30 p.m. Rain fell in torrents during this march. At 10 a.m. the following morning the march was resumed, and proceeding via St. Hilaire and Lillers, we halted in billets for the night at Busnettes. The Battalion was joined en route by 6 Officers and 194 other ranks of the 7th Bn. The King's Own, who had been posted to us on the disbandment of that Battalion. On the 9th, at 9 a.m., we proceeded by march route via Chocques, Annezin, Béthune, Vaudricourt and Drouvin to Houchin, where Camp was reached at 1 p.m. We spent four days in Houchin, where training was resumed while the Commanding Officer, accompanied by the Intelligence Officer and Company Commanders, proceeded to reconnoitre the line, preparatory to the 164th Infantry Brigade taking over La Bassée Canal Sector.

On the 14th February the Battalion paraded, and moved up by Companies at 100 yards interval, to take over position in the Line, as Support Battalion to the Right Sector, and relieved the 6th Lancashire Fusiliers, 42nd Division. On the 20th we relieved the 4th Loyals in the left front Sub-Sector, and spent the time in repairing and improving the trenches. Trench life at this period was comparatively uneventful, quiet periods alternating with intermittent shelling on both sides, while patrols scoured No Man's Land nightly. Pte. Pepper accounted for one of an enemy patrol, who was identified as belonging to " 205 R.I.R.," which useful item of information was duly conveyed to Brigade Headquarters. On the 2nd March the Battalion was relieved by the 5th Lancashire Fusiliers and moved back to Support in the Village Line. On the 5th March we were relieved by portions of the 6th North Staffs. and the 5th South Staffs. Regiment, and moved back by motor lorry to Hingette, where the Battalion was now in Divisional Reserve.

The time was occupied in cleaning up, bathing parades to Béthune, and training under Company arrangements. " Summer " time was adopted at 11 p.m. on the 9th, the clock being put forward an hour. This period was anything but restful ; there was much tension in the air, and the Battalion was under " Stand To " orders in readiness to move to the forward area in case of the expected enemy attack. At 6.10 a.m. on the 11th March, the Battalion received orders to move to the Concentration Area near Gorre, and moved off in fighting order within half an hour of receiving the order. The Battalion, with the remainder of the Brigade, remained in the Concentration Area until 12 noon, when orders were received to move back to Hignette, the orders as to standing-to still remaining in force. A party of Officers and men reconnoitred the ground behind the Portuguese Division on the left, in anticipation of a call to move to the support of that Division. Reveille was now at 4.30 a.m. daily. On the 12th the order to move to the Concentration Area, near Gorre, was received at 6.10 a.m., and within ten minutes the Battalion had moved off. At 10 a.m. we moved back, Headquarters and 2 Companies going into billets at Essars, and 2 Companies to Choqvaux. This state of acute preparation continued, and further reconnoitring of the defences in rear of the Portuguese Division on our left took place. This was a precautionary measure, in the event of orders being received to form a defensive flank if the enemy penetrated the front of that Division.

At 7 a.m. on the 17th, the Battalion moved off by Companies to relieve the 5th King's Liverpool Regt. in the line at Givenchy. The dispositions were as follows : " C " Company left front ; " D " Company right front ; " A " Company in support in Tunnels ; " B " Company in reserve, occupying Givenchy Keep, Mairie Redoubt, and Moat Farm Redoubt. Battalion Headquarters were at South Moor Villas in Hitchen Road. The day was very clear, and nine enemy observation balloons were up, consequently much of our movement was observed, and the whole system was shelled intermittently during the day. Quiet periods alternated with heavy shelling by the enemy, gas shells being largely used, and these mostly of the mustard gas variety. Wolfe Road, King's Road and Windy Corner, in the communication area, in addition to the above mentioned posts, all received these unwelcome attentions. At midnight on the 24th March our Artillery opened a heavy barrage of all calibres, including trench mortars, machine guns, rifle grenades and thermite, on the enemy trenches, and a successful raid was carried out by the 5th King's Liverpool Regt. on our left, and nine prisoners were taken. Enemy retaliation was practically nil. On examination, these prisoners stated that an attack was imminent. In view of this statement the 5th Lancashire Fusiliers were ordered up to the Village Line to strengthen the defences, one Company being attached to our Battalion. Additional Machine Guns were also brought into the Sector, but no attack developed for the time being. On the 27th our snipers had a very successful day, accounting for six of the enemy, including an Officer.

The night was remarkably quiet, and we were relieved by the 5th Lancashire Fusiliers, moving into Brigade Reserve in Gorre. " C " Company occupied the Tuning Fork Line, immediately North of La Bassée Canal. " D " Company took over the Village Line with two Platoons at Pont Fixe, and two Platoons at Windy Corner. Battalion Headquarters and " A " and " B " Companies being in Brigade Reserve in Gorre. The Companies engaged in cleaning up and refitting, also visiting the Divisional Baths at Beuvry. After over a week's perfect weather rain began to fall. At 11.15 a.m. on the 31st March, Church Parade was held at the Château Gorre.

On the 1st April, Companies moved up independently, via the northern bank of La Bassée Canal to Pont Fixe, to relieve the 4th Loyals in the right sector of the Brigade Front on La Bassée Canal. The relief was completed at 11.15 p.m. without incident, the weather being fine, and the night quiet. Dispositions were : Right Front " A " Company ; Centre " B " Company ; Left Front " C " Company ; with " D " Company in support in Givenchy Keeps. Battalion Headquarters were in the Village Line. On the night of the 4th April our Patrols entered the enemy front line and communication trenches without any opposition. Good work on this patrol was done by Second-Lieuts. Raeside, Lyon and Holmes. These patrols again entered the enemy lines on the nights of the 5th and 6th. They penetrated as far as the support line, and found the system unoccupied from the Canal to a point N.E. of Warlingham Crater. A raid which should have been undertaken by the 4th Loyals was cancelled, owing to information gained by our Patrols. The 8th was a very quiet day. Not a shell fell on the Brigade front. " D " Company in the Keeps relieved " C " Company on the left front.

On the morning of the 9th April there was a heavy fog. The enemy opened a bombardment with gas shells, and a few 4.2's and 5.9's, behind our front line. Gradually gas shelling decreased, and the volume of heavier shells increased, the front line receiving some attention. The following brief summary of events, altogether inadequate to the occasion, must unhappily suffice to give some indication of the historic stand now made by the 55th (West Lancashire) Division, against what was to be the last main despairing effort of a formidable enemy to overwhelm his opponent :—

7.30 *a.m.*—Our front line was destroyed by Minenwerfers, and shelling was very heavy on Oxford Terrace and Bayswater.

8.5 *a.m.*—Battalion Headquarters was very heavily shelled, and caused serious casualties to Headquarters, Runners and Pioneers.

9.30 *a.m.*—An " S.O.S." was received by Runner from Canal North, despatched at 9.15 by Captain Ellwood. This was transmitted by power buzzer, and also by Runner, to the forward guns, and to Brigade.

10.30 *a.m.*—Bayswater from Cheyne Walk to 100 yards north were held by us. 5th Lancashire Fusiliers from Support reached the Village Line. One Platoon of " C " Company, 5th Lancashire Fusiliers reinforced main line of resistance. " D " Company, 5th Lancashire Fusiliers formed a defensive flank at Windy Corner, where the enemy had broken through the Portuguese Division on our left as anticipated. The enemy was prevented from penetrating west of Pont Pike—Windy Corner.

10.50 *a.m.*—" A " Company were back at Spoil Bank, and re-took Company Headquarters and Cheyne Walk to beyond Bayswater. Bayswater was cleared by bombing, and Death or Glory Sap was still holding out.

10.55 *a.m.*—Mairie Redoubt was still intact, and Gunner Siding N. held, the enemy being bombed out of Gunner Siding S. towards Orchard Road. We were in touch with the 4th Loyals on our left.

11.20 *a.m.*—No sign of enemy at Mairie Redoubt. Our right Company was in touch with 5th Lancashire Fusiliers in Bayswater, who bombed up Orchard Road.

12.5 *p.m.*—Enemy holding top of Orchard Road and firing machine guns across Spoil Bank.

12.15 *p.m.*—We took 14 prisoners in Death or Glory Sap.

12.55 *p.m.*—Enemy still in Orchard Keep.

3 *p.m.*—Enemy in Company Headquarters, in Oxford Terrace, Gunner Trench cleared by Captain Evans and Captain Overton.

3.20 *p.m.*—Company Headquarters in Oxford Terrace re-taken, and enemy cleared from Bayswater and Oxford Terrace.

3.35 *p.m.*—Enemy cleared from Orchard Keep.

4 *p.m.*—Enemy cleared from Cheyne Walk, Bayswater and Spoil Bank. Oxford and Cambridge Terrace reported all clear. Reorganization of Keeps in progress.

4.50 *p.m.*—Arrival of 2 Officers and 50 other ranks, details of other Units, as reinforcements.

4.55 *p.m.*—Situation on Battalion front : " A " Company in occupation of Bayswater and Death or or Glory Sap. " B " Company in occupation of Bayswater (with 17 other ranks). " C " Company in occupation of Oxford Terrace (with one attached Platoon of 5th Lancashire Fusiliers), Mairie Redoubt, Gunner Siding and Orchard Keep. " D " Company in occupation of Cambridge Terrace to Wolfe Road. Enemy in occupation of Warlingham Crater and Lower Finchley Road.

5 *p.m.*—One Company of 5th South Lancashire Regiment (Captain Hill) arrives, and is divided between " A " and " C " Companies.

7.20 *p.m.*—Mairie Redoubt, Orchard Keep, and Gunner Siding normally held by us.

April 10*th*, 12.30 *a.m.*—Our original line now held intact. A Patrol of the right front Company reports no enemy movement in No Man's Land or enemy front line trenches. The night was quiet, with no Artillery fire, and little machine gun fire.

9.40 *a.m.*—Enemy Aeroplane No. 18 dropped a bomb on Bayswater, wounding 14 of " A " Company. Our low-flying planes fired into enemy trenches. During the afternoon the enemy shelled Windy Corner —Pont Fixe very heavily with 4.2, 5.9, and 8-in. (or 11-in.) shells. Observation of movement behind the enemy lines leads to expectation of another hostile attack. We opened a harassing Artillery and Machine Gun fire on the enemy front line, which continued until 9 p.m. and then slackened.

11*th April*.—Patrols out during the night of 10th/11th April reported no hostile occupation of No Man's Land, and no sound of movement of troops. There was no enemy activity during the night, beyond occasional long bursts of machine gun fire from Embankment Redoubt and from North East. The afternoon was quiet, but there was a violent bombardment of Le Plantin in the evening.

11.10 *p.m.*—Relief of " D " Company in the left Sector, by " C " Coy. in the Keeps, was reported complete, but this relief was considerably delayed by shell fire.

12*th April*, 9.30 *a.m.*—The Brigade Major visited Battalion Headquarters and issued verbal orders for the relief of the Battalion in the Line, by the 5th Lancashire Fusiliers from the Village Line. Operation Orders were issued, and reconnaissances of dispositions were carried out at once.

1 *p.m.*—Relief commenced and was successfully carried out by small parties.

6.35 *p.m.*—Relief completed. Dispositions now in the Village Line were : Pont Fixe, " A " Company (with " D " Company, 5th South Lancashire Regiment). Fanshawe Castle, " D " and " B " Companies. Windy Corner, " C " Company. Battalion Headquarters remained unchanged.

13*th April*.—The enemy bombarded the Village Line during the day, and the work of wiring the northern flank between Windy Corner and Lone Farm commenced.

14*th April*, 4.45 *p.m.*—The Windy Corner defences were taken over from " C " Company, by a Company of the 5th South Lancashire Regiment. Information was received of the forthcoming relief of the Brigade by the 1st Brigade.

15*th April*.—Preparations for relief by the 1st Camerons.

16*th April*, 11 *a.m.*—Lewis Gun Teams of the 1st Camerons arrived at Westminster Bridge, and were conducted by guides to Companies.

10 *p.m.*—Relieving Companies met at Westminster Bridge.

11.15 *p.m.*—Relief completed without incident. Enemy Artillery was quiet during the relief. Companies proceeded independently to a point on the

Beuvry—Béthune Road, where buses were waiting to convey them to their destination. During this operation a dozen 5.9 shells fell in the vicinity, but had no effect beyond accelerating the departure of the convoy. The Company of the 5th South Lancashire Regiment left us here, and proceeded to Burbure.

One episode in this outstanding engagement may be commented on. Orchard Keep—a key position—was occupied by 2nd Lieut. J. H. Collin and sixteen Non Commissioned Officers and men, who held the post until overwhelmed by successive attacks by the Germans. The whole of this party were reported killed, but Lance-Corporal J. Pollitt was wounded and taken prisoner. Badly wounded as he was, this N.C.O. killed his escort, and fought his way back alone to our lines. The defence of Orchard Keep made such an impression on the Higher Command that 2nd Lieut. J. H. Collin was awarded the posthumous Victoria Cross (see Appendix). It therefore seems reasonable to assume that Lance-Corpl. Pollitt, as the only survivor of this very gallant band, was an unlucky victim of the fortune of war, in that he received no official recognition of his valuable services on this and other occasions. It is interesting too, that Lance-Corpl. Pollitt was associated with the events which led to the grant of the two Victoria Crosses previously earned by the Battalion.

The Battalion arrived in billets in Marles-les-Mines at 4 a.m. on the 17th. These billets were comfortable and much appreciated. The usual daily parades followed, and these included bathing parades to Auchel, and visits to the 55th Divisional Theatre at the same village. On the 21st April at 10 a.m., the Battalion paraded and marched, accompanied by the Band, to the Aerodrome near Auchel, where an inspection of the Brigade by the Divisional Commander was held. It was anticipated that the French Premier would be present at this parade, but for some reason of State, this anticipation was not realised. At 6.30 a.m. on the 23rd, the Battalion proceeded by bus to Vaudricourt, in the Houchin area, prior to taking over trenches again. Here, as the weather was delightfully sunny, the day was spent agreeably in the woods. In the evening two Companies moved off by the light railway, to relieve the 1st Battalion The Loyals in the Givenchy Sector, while two Companies and Battalion Headquarters moved up by bus. Headquarters sustained 10 casualties through Artillery fire, when alighting near Annequin. Dispositions were as follows : Right Sector, La Bassée Canal ; on the right, " A " Company ; centre, " B " Company ; left, " C " Company, with " D " Company in support. The Transport moved to the Château Drouvin.

Two of our fighting patrols, which went out just after dark on the 25th, to occupy the junction of Orchard Road and front line, to the junction of Finchley Road and front line, met the enemy in force, became heavily engaged, and were driven back. Second-Lieuts. Sykes and Whitmore were wounded. A barrage was put down to enable a third party to rush this line. The barrage came down in No Man's Land, behind the objective, and our men could not advance against hostile machine gun fire. Several casualties were sustained. The enemy were holding our old front line in strength. At 4 a.m. on the 26th April, covered by Artillery fire, two platoons of " A " and " D " Companies rushed the enemy position, and heavy hand-to-hand fighting ensued. Our party was forced to withdraw. At 2.20 p.m., under cover of Artillery fire and Machine Gun barrage, two Platoons of " C " and " D " Companies attempted, in conjunction with 5th Lancashire Fusiliers to retake the crater saps on our left. The barrage did not come down on " K " and " J " Saps, and the Lancashire Fusiliers were unable to reach their objectives. The 4th King's Own reached their objectives after fierce fighting, during which 40 German prisoners were taken. Parties of " C " Company, under Second-Lieut. Hunter, on the left, quickly cleared Berkeley Street, " E " Sap, and front line. Parties of " D " Company, under Second-Lieut. Stewart, on the right, rushed from Coventry Sap and took " A " Sap, also obtaining touch with " C " Company. Second-Lieut. Hunter was killed after these objectives were reached. Touch was established with the 5th Lancashire Fusiliers but the latter were driven from their positions by strong enemy counter attacks. Our own posts became surrounded on three sides, and we were forced to give ground. After bitter fighting we accomplished a successful withdrawal to our former lines, after inflicting heavy losses on the enemy. Congratulations were received from Corps, Division, and Brigade Commanders on the fine fighting qualities displayed.

On the 28th April we were relieved by the 4th Loyals, and went into support in the Village Line, Battalion Headquarters being in Fanshawe Castle ; " B " and " D " Companies in Canal Bank ; " A " Company in Pont Fixe, and " C " Company, Windy Corner. The 7th King's Liverpool Regt. relieved us on the night of the 1st May, and we went into Brigade Reserve in Verquigneul, where re-clothing, refitting and bathing was carried out. Reinforcements joined us and Companies were reorganized. The Divisional Commander inspected and interviewed parties of " C " and " D " Companies who took part in the recent attack on the Crater Saps. Platoon and Company training were also carried out. On the 8th May preparations were made for going up into the line. 2 Officers and 135 other ranks proceeded by march route to Allouagne, to Corps Reinforcement Depot, as " B " Team. At 7.30 p.m. the march to the trenches by platoons commenced. We relieved the 5th King's Liverpool Regt. in the Givenchy Right Sector, Left Sub-Sector. The relief was completed at 1.40 a.m. on the 9th without incident. Dispositions were as follows : left front, " A " Company ; centre, " D " Company ; right front, " B " Company ; " C " Company in support in the Keeps. There was much enemy activity during this tour of duty in the trenches, especially by his Artillery, and also in the air. On the 14th May a low flying aeroplane was engaged by our machine guns, and shortly afterwards the enemy's artillery, searching from Pont Fixe to

Windy Corner, succeeded in blowing up an ammunition store at the latter post.

Such was the general position at this time. Outwardly, the course of events, for the next three or four months, followed the same routine. Life alternated between the trenches at Givenchy, and Reserve at Drouvin Camp. It is earnestly hoped that a cursory glance at the period under review, will not convey the impression that nothing worthy of note was happening. Far from it ; but a closer analysis would be a repetition of what has already been presented to the reader. The Battalion underwent its usual hazardous tour of duty in the trenches, and close proximity to the enemy could never be uneventful. It will be recalled that during the strong attack by the Germans on April 9th, we were compelled to retire slightly from our old front line, and this had since been occupied by the enemy. This line was accordingly re-occupied by our troops, and a great quantity of salvage was found and brought down.

The spirit which now prevailed amongst our troops was restrained optimism. This feeling had an intangible quality, gossamer in texture, more tacit than expressed, but everywhere radiating good cheer, and hope for the near future. The power of the enemy's attack appeared to have been definitely broken, while the time was approaching when our own irresistible advance was to reach a triumphant conclusion.

On the 21st August, at Vaudricourt, we listened to a lecture by Brigadier-General G. I. Stockwell, telling us about, and explaining a secret attack on the Craters, to be carried out by the 5th Lancashire Fusiliers and ourselves, and Officers and N.C.O.s studied a model of the Craters. The following day this lecture was repeated to the men by Company Commanders. Preparations for the coming attack were made, and great keenness was shewn. On the 23rd August we moved up the line to assembly positions, with Headquarters in the Givenchy Tunnel. The Battalion was very busy making final arrangements.

At 2-20 a.m. on the morning of the 24th August, all Companies were in assembly positions. Despite a very slight harassing fire no casualties were sustained. Wire cutting had previously been carried out by advance parties. The enemy was very quiet, sent up few lights, and showed no signs of anticipating an attack. Supporting Companies received hot breakfasts, and the assembling troops had sandwiches and chocolate. No noise was made in getting up food. Snipers crept out to position on spoil heaps, from which they kept down enemy observation prior to the attack, and kept down enemy fire during the attack, by firing on such targets as exposed themselves.

At 6 a.m. visibility became very poor, a slight rain falling. Our own Stokes Mortars fired intermittently on the crater areas up to the time when the rockets were fired at zero hour. One of our aeroplanes flew low over the craters, drawing only a very slight machine gun fire. On the firing of the rockets at 7.20 a.m., the assaulting troops immediately advanced under splendid leadership. Two and a half minutes elapsed before the enemy fired his first rifle shot. There was no artillery fire at all. The enemy was completely taken by surprise, and was found mostly in dugouts. Not a single enemy machine gun was in action on the Battalion front. At 7.24 a.m. an S.O.S. rocket, bursting into two red lights, was fired from well behind the enemy's lines. Meanwhile, mopping up parties had followed closely behind the front line of sections, but found the enemy to be in small strength. These were effectively dealt with, some being killed and some being taken prisoner. A few tried to run away but were heavily fired on.

At 7.30 a.m. our own protective barrage fell beyond the crater area, this being answered three minutes later by a poor counter barrage directed chiefly on Gunner Siding. At 7.35 a.m. Companies had reached their objectives on the far lip of the craters, and telephone communication was established between them and Battalion Headquarters. At 7.43 a.m.

consolidation was immediately proceeded with. Up to this time casualties were practically nil. Patrols were sent out to deal with Trench Mortar emplacements, and one was reported destroyed by mobile charge by the Left Company. Our own barrage, which was very heavy, seems to have dropped some shells short, inflicting casualties, two men being killed and 8 wounded in the Left Company, and approximately the same number in the Right Company.

Enemy retaliation dwindled down to very slight proportions between 8-30 and 10-30 a.m. He did not appear to know on what points to fire. At 8.34 a.m. a message was received from the snipers that a party of nearly forty of the enemy were seen at the far end of Duck Bill extension. These were fired on and soon disappeared. Shortly afterwards news was received from the Australian Tunnellers to the effect that there were no mines in dugouts, and that all shelters were badly smashed, a pill box in Red Dragon Crater alone being untouched. Parties of the enemy in small numbers were seen running to the rear, and were dealt with by Lewis Gunners and Snipers, those escaping getting right into our barrage. At 9.20 a.m. consolidation was reported to be making good progress, while communication trenches were being rapidly dug by Pioneers, from Wolfe Road to Berkeley Street.

At 9.40 a.m. an S.O.S. rocket was sent up from the area of the left Battalion. Enemy Artillery was not firing at all at the time. Five minutes later the S.O.S. was cancelled.

Shortly afterwards the enemy fired on the crater area for the first time, on Warlinghem. Owing to our own Artillery fire some patrols had difficulty in reaching Trench Mortar emplacements, and these were now sent out again. The Right Company reported reaching an emplacement, but found the Mortar gone, though plenty of very heavy ammunition, and a range finder were lying near. The Left Company reported the destruction of another emplacement.

Between 11 and 11.15 a.m. enemy Artillery became much more active, blue cross shells falling on Givenchy, and the gas drifting over our area. This had cleared by 11.45 a.m. From this time onwards, much heavier enemy barrages were put down on the crater area. Tea and sandwiches were got up to the front line troops about 12.30 p.m., and about an hour later, a hot meat meal. Considerable difficulty was experienced in getting rations over the broken ground to the crater area, and the work done by the Transport and Quarter-Master's Department was commendable. Perhaps a smile may be permitted here. This devoted personnel, its duty well and truly done, assembled for departure from the inhospitable region of the craters, which the Hun was now freely shelling. One member of the party was missing, and he the Company Quarter-Master Sergeant. Impatience grew as the minutes passed, and when well nigh insupportable, he appeared, to meet the indignant queries of his comrades, he silenced criticism with the explanation " Well, I couldn't find t' dixie lid " !

Our casualties during these operations amounted to 30, viz. : 7 killed and 23 wounded. On the 25th and 26th August the new line was organized. Difficulty was experienced by our Patrols in getting into touch with the enemy, and it was not until the second day that his posts were found. Our Snipers did excellent work, getting three confirmed hits, and continually harassing the enemy in his broken communication trenches. On the 27th we were relieved by the 5th King's Liverpool Regt. without incident, and went into billets at Drovbin Camp, arriving shortly after 9 p.m.

News of a German retirement on the front of the 15th Division, reached Battalion Headquarters astride La Bassée Canal, at 10 a.m. on the 2nd October. In consequence of this information, daylight patrols were sent out by " A " and " B " Companies, these Companies holding the right half of the Brigade Outpost Line. The advanced Platoons of " B " Company, under Lieut. Peers, were, on this morning, occupying

Canteleux Trench, from its junction with Canteleux Alley S., to Towpath Alley, with forward posts in shell holes. " A " Company, to the south of the Canal, had taken over, the previous evening, the dispositions of three Companies of the 4th Loyals, who had captured the Distillery, viz., a line of posts 200 yards East of the Distillery Line, with supporting and counter attack platoons in rear. The two counter attack platoons were attached from " D " Company.

Progress was first made by " B " Company, one of whose patrols had entered La Bassée Line before mid-day. By 1.30 p.m. the western outskirts of La Bassée were reached, and at 2 p.m. patrols were pushing North up the front and support trenches of La Bassée line, to gain touch with the 5th Lancashire Fusiliers who were advancing towards La Bassée from the direction of Canteleux and Violaines. Opposite their front, however, the enemy seemed to hold his line normally, until mid-day, and even later.

Shortly after 1 o'clock, Lieut. Rudall (" A " Company) had entered without opposition, La Bassée line S. of the Canal, and was pushing S. down the trench to gain touch with patrols which were working their way along Vert Alley. At 2.30 we were in occupation of La Bassée line, from the Canal to Vert Alley, and had gained touch with the 16th Division. Instructions were then received from the Brigadier General Commanding 164th Infantry Brigade to hold La Bassée Line with two Platoons, and push into Le Faubourg to Canal Basin and Crassiers. Meantime patrols of " B " Company had pushed through La Bassée, and reached at 4.30 p.m., a point 800 yards East of it. Major R. Gardner, M.C., under whose command this advance guard was operating, then left Battalion Headquarters at Spoil Bank, and at 5 p.m. established Headquarters of the Right Advance Guard at the Distillery. He was accompanied by Lieut. Tucker (Intelligence Officer), and by a few Signallers and Runners. Communications with Spoil Bank were at first maintained by telephone, via one of the other Company Headquarters. On the establishment of Battalion Headquarters at Canteleux at 7 p.m., communications became very precarious, as the wire over the Canal became " dissed " by the blowing up of a barge. A " loop set," however, was fixed up at the Distillery, with which efforts were made to get into touch with a similar instalment in Red Dragon Crater. Telephone communication, however, with the Company Headquarters already referred to, was maintained.

Patrols had by 5 o'clock, reached Crassiers, and located the enemy. Patrols elsewhere were also pushing on, in touch with the 16th Division. Two Platoons from " B " Company then crossed the Canal, and were disposed in La Bassée Line, which was temporarily held as the main line of resistance. By 8 p.m. outposts were established along an advanced line, and Vanguard Headquarters were in La Bassée, in a concrete cellar. From a reconnaissance of the Canal it was observed that the bridges had been totally destroyed. It was, however, just possible to scramble over near the remains of the old railway bridge. There was no sign of any footbridge along the Canal. Road reconnaissance showed that the main Annequin—La Bassée road was fit for horse and motor traffic as far as Le Faubourg. Roads towards Canal Basin from Le Faubourg were also good for horse traffic ; that running south towards Cité de Douvrin was not so good.

The only opposition to our Patrols came from a machine gun. This, however, ceased before dusk, and a party of 20 of the enemy were seen marching thence towards Salomé in full marching order. Before midnight a post was established in the Old Brewery on the Salomé Road, and another south of the Canal. Detachments of Machine Gunners (55th Division Machine Gun Battalion, 4 Guns ; 16th Division Machine Gun Battalion, 2 Guns), Stokes Mortars, Lewis Gunners, and Investigation Parties had all reported at Advanced Guard Headquarters at the Distillery by 8 p.m. About midnight two patrols were sent out to push forward into Salomé, one along the N. and the other along the S. side of the Canal, and establish a post in Salomé, in touch with each other. These posts were established by 2 a.m. on the 3rd October. A patrol also went down the road to gain touch with the Division on the right.

Salomé was found deserted—the enemy had completely disappeared—and touch was gained with a patrol of the 5th Lancashire Fusiliers in Salomé. At 7 a.m. the line of resistance of the Advance Guard was moved forward to a general line, with forward posts and two supporting platoons. A patrol reached the Canal angle, and further patrols were sent to reconnoitre Berclau. Billy Berclau was found to have been reached by the 16th Division, and touch was established with their left post. At 10.55 a.m. Billy Berclau was lightly shelled by the enemy, and at the same time Machine Gun and Anti-Aircraft Artillery fire was observed from Berclau. Advance Guard Headquarters was established near the Canal Basin, whither the " loop set " from the Distillery was removed. This was picked up by the " loop set " of the forward Brigade, and communication with our Brigade was thus obtained. In other directions visual signalling was resorted to.

Four machine guns were disposed in the main line of resistance, 2 were maintained in reserve at Headquarters. One Stokes Mortar was also conveyed by mule to the Vanguard Headquarters. A forward dump of 57 boxes of small arm ammunition was established in rear of the main line of resistance. Cooking was done in La Bassée, and the men supplied with hot food during the day. Cross-country communications from La Bassée to the outpost line of resistance was easy, the tracks being undamaged. At 1 p.m. a post was reported established in Berclau, but later an enemy rearguard was located in another part of the village. Fighting took place, and our post was compelled to withdraw. The N. and N.E. outskirts of Berclau were found strongly held by machine guns and snipers. We established a Lewis Gun Post which commanded Berclau.

At 4.45 p.m. orders were received from Brigade to arrange for the 16th Division to take over the dispositions of the Right Advance Guard, owing to a change of boundaries. The southern boundary of our Brigade was fixed on the line of the Canal—Canal Angle—Canal Tee. The Advance Guard, and all attached troops were to move to assembly positions in Salomé, N. of the Canal, and await the remainder of the 4th King's Own, which was coming up from La Bassée, to relieve the 5th Lancashire Fusiliers in the Brigade Outpost line, on the night of the 3rd/4th October, and to continue the advance on the morning of the 4th. At 7.30 p.m. Advance Guard Headquarters closed and crossed the Canal. Major R. Gardner, M.C., the Commander, reported at Battalion Headquarters in Salomé at 9 p.m. The outpost platoons and attached troops crossed the Canal, and spent the night in billets in Salomé. The whole Battalion, under the command of Lieut.-Colonel G. B. Balfour, D.S.O., now acted as Advance Guard to the Brigade.

On the morning of the 4th October, patrols pushed forward at dawn from Hantay, and drove the enemy back to the Canal. A good deal of patrol fighting took place. " D " Company attacked and took Prevore Farm. The enemy held the western bank of the Canal and bridgeheads with machine guns. The 18-pr. Battery attached to the Advance Guard, shelled the bridgeheads and the Laundry. On the 5th October, patrols continued to drive the enemy back, but could not get across the Haute Deule Canal, which he was holding strongly. The enemy flooded the area in front of the Canal, and caused our patrols and posts to withdraw a short distance. The Battalion was relieved during the night by the 6th King's Liverpools and marched back to Divisional Reserve in the vicinity of Pont Fixe and Givenchy, with Battalion Headquarters at Barge House. Here we rested, bathed and refitted. The weather was wet, and there were no working parties. Companies were not very comfortable in dugouts, and on the 7th the Battalion moved back to billets in Beuvry. Here training in Advance Guards was carried out, and kits and stores were again reduced to the lowest minimum, so as to conform to the transport available.

On the 11th October one Officer per Company reconnoitred the left Brigade front (166th Brigade), with a view to taking over the following day. A demonstration in rapid pontoon bridging was given in the afternoon. This followed a lecture in the morning by the Divisional Educational Officer on the scheme for education *on the cessation of hostilities.* This encouraged impressions not to be ignored, and if the general spirit of the troops was exuberant, it was based on solid foundation and not mere flimsy excuse. Much remained to be done, however, and on the 12th October the Battalion left Beuvry in trains at 8.30 a.m. to relieve the 10th Liverpool Scottish in the forward area. There were two collisions on the way but no one was hurt. We detrained at Cambrin, and marched to the neighbourhood of Marquillies, where Battalion Headquarters were established. " A " Company in Marquillies ; " B " Company in Sainghin ; " C " Company in Le Willy, and " D " Company in the Sugar Factory. Relief was completed at 5 p.m. without any special incident.

On the following day posts were dug and wired all round. There was a good deal of shelling but no casualties were sustained. On the 14th, Battalion Headquarters moved to a house near the Sugar Factory. Two Companies were in the main line of resistance, and two in support. We supplied one working party, and Officers reconnoitred the forward area.

On the 17th the Battalion left Sainghin, moving off at 9 a.m., and marched by Companies through Wavrin to Lattre. There was some delay in crossing the Canal at Seclin, owing to the bridges being blown up. We then moved on to Ancoisne, where a mid-day meal was served. Here we met the first released civilians, and our reception was most cordial. About

2 p.m. the Battalion moved on to Houplines, and were still under orders to advance. At 6.30 p.m. we arrived at Templemars, remaining there for the night. Our reception here was even more cordial than before. Battalion Headquarters were established at the Mayor's house. At 6 a.m. on the 18th, the Battalion moved off to pass through the 5th Lancashire Fusiliers. "C" and "D" were Outpost Companies, with "A" and "B" Companies in support. The patrols pushed on and entered Peronne. The enemy were holding the bank of the river La Marque in considerable strength, and there was a good deal of shelling, the fort at Sainghin, and Peronne, being the chief targets. Bas Sainghin caused "D" Company a good deal of trouble, and it was not until the afternoon that it was cleared. A heavy mist hung over the area of operations, and greatly assisted us in moving forward. The night was very light, with a brilliant moon. By means of a ladder, "D" Company patrol was able to cross La Marque, and enter Bouvines. At 10.30 p.m. we put down a machine gun barrage, also our 18-pr. Batteries fired on woods where the enemy were located. This seems to have forced the enemy to retire before he intended, and he finally left the village at 11.15 p.m. Our reception by the villagers was most cordial.

On the 19th October, the whole Outpost Line pushed out, and by the early morning our line was established on the railway line east of Bouvines, and patrols had entered Cysoing. The 4th Loyals now passed through us, and our Battalion concentrated in Bouvines for a rest. During the early morning "B" Company had captured 23 prisoners and 3 machine guns. Headquarters were established in a Château, and everyone was very comfortable. The villagers were overjoyed at their deliverance, and did all they could to make the troops comfortable. The bridge across the river had been blown up, and the villagers helped the Royal Engineers to build a new one, which was completed by 11.30 a.m.

The Battalion left Bouvines at 8.30 a.m. on the 20th to take over the role of "B" Battalion. We

K   *Page* 129

passed through Cysoing at 10 a.m. and marched to Creplain, where we halted. The Battalion then moved on again to the area around the Ferme du Baron, north of Froidmont, where we again halted and awaited orders. The next move was to a field about 800 yards north of Esplechin, where we formed up into Artillery formation. " D " Company was sent to support the left flank of the 5th Lancashire Fusiliers, and one Platoon to obtain touch with the 74th Division on our left. At 6 p.m. Battalion Headquarters moved to a farm in Esplechin, and " A " and " B " Companies moved to support the right flank of the 5th Lancashire Fusiliers. The remaining three Platoons of " C " Company moved to the left, and joined " D " Company, thus the whole Battalion was now in the Support Line. Battalion Headquarters moved to the Asylum in Froidmont, and were cordially greeted by the jovial Brothers of Charity.

On the 21st October, the Battalion passed through the 5th Lancashire Fusiliers, but found progress well contested by the enemy. Severe patrol fighting took place. The high ground on the road from Froidmont to Tournai was captured by " B " Company at 3.15 p.m., but was retaken by the enemy at 10 p.m. On the right, considerable opposition was met with in Ere, and a machine gun was located, firing from the Church. The Church itself was mined. The enemy were finally pushed beyond Ere, and we took up a line about 500 yards beyond the village. Ere was heavily shelled during the day and night. At 7 p.m. Headquarters moved to the Château near Ere, and an advanced Headquarters was established in Ere. The enemy appeared to be making a stand on the north side of the river Scheldt. The shelling was severe, and all the sunken roads were marked down for harassing fire. During the morning of the 22nd, the 5th Loyals took over our line, and the Battalion took over a battle line in support. " D " Company had some casualties when coming out of the Outpost Line. The Battalion rested during the day. " A " Company were gassed rather heavily at 6 p.m., but suffered no casualties.

On the 23rd October the Battalion was holding the Battle Line, the men being as far as possible in farm houses, within easy reach of posts to be manned in case of S.O.S. At 4.45 p.m., in conjunction with the 14th Black Watch (late Fife and Forfar Yeomanry), one platoon of " D " Company attacked a sunken road, but without success. Enemy machine gun fire was very intense, and the men could only advance to within 100 yards of the trench, when the Officer and 5 men were wounded. The men were collected together by the Platoon Sergeant, and formed posts on the eastern edge of a wood, about 150 yards from the objective. The remainder of the Battalion were making posts. On the 24th Companies were engaged in digging V-shaped trenches, about 40 yards long, and these were inspected by the Commanding Officer during the morning. This work was carried out until 2 a.m. on the 25th, when 15 such trenches had been completed. Battalion Headquarters were moved to the farm house Du Baron during the afternoon, and Companies were billeted in farms in the vicinity.

During the morning of the 25th October, " D " Company (Reserve Company) carried on with the construction of the trenches. The Battalion was relieved in the main line of resistance about 5 p.m. by the 4th Loyals, and, on relief, moved forward and relieved the 5th Lancashire Fusiliers in the Outpost Line. Battalion Headquarters were established in the Tannery. " B " and " C " Companies held the front line, with " A " and " D " Companies in support. Second-Lieut. A. Rigg was here wounded in the leg by a machine gun bullet. The Battalion and the 4th Loyals now became attached to the 165th Infantry Brigade. On the 26th October the Battalion had the misfortune to lose the further services of the Commanding Officer, Lieut.-Colonel G. B. Balfour, D.S.O., who, along with Lieut. H. Tucker, went to hospital, sick. Colonel Balfour had the distinguished honour of serving with the Battalion throughout the War, from the time when he mobilised as a Lieutenant in August, 1914. The Command of the Battalion devolved upon Major R. Gardner, M.C., who was promoted Acting Lieut.-Colonel, and who himself had proceeded to France with the Battalion and had rendered most valuable service.

Ere Church and vicinity were continually harassed during the day with gas shells and whizbangs. An aeroplane, belonging to " C " Flight, was shot down, but was salvaged intact from No Man's Land by " A " Company. During the morning another of our aeroplanes was forced to land, with a bullet through the tank, near Pic-au-Vent, the pilot and observer being uninjured. On the whole, the Battalion had a quiet day.

At 5.30 a.m. on the 27th the Royal Air Force took away in a lorry the first aeroplane we salvaged the previous day. During the morning there was a slight gas shelling of Pic-au-Vent, Croix-de-Pierre, and Ere Church, but the Battalion had a quiet day in the Line. On the 29th an enemy aeroplane was brought down on the right of the Battalion front. The observer was seen to descend by means of a parachute, and was taken prisoner by the 10th Liverpool Scottish on the right. The Battalion had a quiet day in the Line, and was relieved at 7.30 p.m. by the 6th King's Liverpool Regt. On relief, the Battalion proceeded to billets in Bourchelles. Here the opportunity was taken of cleaning up, paying the men, and bathing at Cysoing. Succeeding days were devoted to training in open warfare, and Colonel Gardner addressed the Battalion on the parade ground. Capt. A. E. Morton, M.C., Lieuts. H. Lauder and Steeple, and Second-Lieut. I. G. Anderson rejoined the Battalion here, whilst by way of recreation, a dance was given in the village school, with the Battalion Band in attendance, and which proved very popular. There were also some fine Cinema shows given in the same building from time to time. The weather was not too kind at this time, rain being rather persistent.

On the 8th November, the Battalion received orders to be prepared to move at short notice, and everything was prepared in readiness for this, the remainder of the day being devoted to training in billets, the day being very wet. At 1 a.m. on the 9th we received orders to move to Esplechin, and at 9.50 a.m. the Battalion proceeded to that village by march route, arriving at 11.30 a.m., and now came under the orders of the 166th Infantry Brigade. On the 10th November, at 5.30 a.m., we received orders to move forward towards Leuze, and proceeded by march route at 6.45 a.m. The route taken was via Froidmont—Ere—Pontrieu—Vaulx—Les Tournai, along the main Tournai—Ath Road to Leuze, where the Battalion arrived at 7 p.m. Progress on the march was considerably delayed, owing to the main road being blown up by mines in many places. We found good billets in Leuze, and were very comfortable for the night, the inhabitants giving the Battalion a most cordial reception. We received orders from the 166th Infantry Brigade to move forward next morning at 11 a.m.

At 10.45 a.m. on the 11th November, the Battalion formed up in mass on the Square at Leuze, preparatory to moving forward. A few minutes before 11 o'clock the Commanding Officer, Lieut.-Colonel R. Gardner, M.C., read out on parade, a telegram, received from the 166th Infantry Brigade, stating that an Armistice had been signed by Germany, and that hostilities would cease at 11 a.m. A Squadron of the 1st Royal Dragoons, being then in Leuze, on their way forward, also formed up in the Square, and at 11 o'clock sounded the Cavalry " Cease Fire." The Battalion then gave a Royal Salute, and the Band played the National Anthems of England, Belgium, and France. We then moved forward, amid great cheering from the civilian population, and proceeded along the main road to Ligne, where a halt was made, and the Battalion had lunch. Orders were received here from the 164th Infantry Brigade to proceed to Villers St. Amand, where we duly arrived about 2.45 p.m. Billets were obtained, and the Battalion rested here for the night, coming again under the orders of the 164th Infantry Brigade.

CHAPTER IX.

CONCLUSION.

Little remains to be told. The great conflict was over, with overwhelming victory on our side. What followed might have been of importance and interest in the ordinary peace time experience of the Battalion but, after its searching test of the past four years, current events assumed the complexion of the commonplace and even dull. What will always remain of imperishable importance and interest, is that the Battalion emerged from its trials with jealously guarded reputation untarnished, and fit to hand on to successors, as an incentive to maintain the high standard of the 4th King's Own Royal Regt.

On Sunday, 17th November, 8 Officers attended a solemn Te Deum in Ath, and the Battalion took part in a combined Church of England and Nonconformist Thanksgiving Service. On the 18th we moved to Chappelle-a-Wattines, and became attached to the 271st Company R.E., for work on stripping railways. This was varied by football and organized games, concerts, and liberal leave to visit Ath. On the 7th December a Guard of Honour was furnished to mark the passing of His Majesty the King, to whom the Brigadier General Commanding was presented. On the 15th December the Battalion left Leuze, and by a series of marches via Ath—Enghein—Buysinghem, reached Uccle, near Brussels, where we arrived on the 18th, after a few days' march. Christmas Day in Uccle was seasonably marked by attending Church Parade in the morning. This was followed by the men's dinner at 1 o'clock, and the Sergeants' dinner at 6 o'clock. In the afternoon the Battalion Football Team played the champion Belgian Team, on the latter's ground, the game ending in a draw of 2 goals each. The men enjoyed themselves, and everybody spent a very happy Christmas Day.

On the 3rd January, 1919, the Division was inspected by the General Officer Commanding, on the third anniversary of its formation.   The Division was drawn up on the road running through Bois-de-Cambre. The G.O.C. and Staff rode down the line, and afterwards the Earl of Derby, K.G., motored slowly over the same course.   The Division, led by the 4th King's Own Regt., as the senior Regiment of the Division, marched past in fours, the salute being taken by H.M. The King of the Belgians.   The Belgians attending the ceremony were very enthusiastic, especially when the Colours passed the saluting base.   The Colours were carried on this occasion by Lieut. Tucker and Second-Lieut. Dane, M.C.   On the 26th January, H.M. The King of the Belgians reviewed the III Corps Troops, to which we belonged.   The march through Brussels commenced at the Avenue Louise, and proceeded to the Place des Palais, where the salute was taken by King Albert.   Their Royal Highnesses The Prince of Wales and Prince Albert were both present at the ceremony.

Life in and around Brussels at this period was very agreeable.   Many Concerts and Dances were given, and proved most popular.   Meanwhile heavy drafts were being prepared, and despatched to the Army of Occupation at Bonn, and to England on demobilization.   This so reduced the strength that no training was possible, all the men being employed in special capacities, and on guard duties.   On the 24th February the Battalion was reorganised as two Companies—the Cadre Company and the Rhine Draft Company—the total strength being now under 200.   The Regimental Colours were removed from the Officers' Mess, and handed over to the Quarter-Master for safe custody. On the 12th March, Brigadier-General G. I. Stockwell, C.B., C.M.G., D.S.O., relinquished the Command of the 164th Infantry Brigade, on being appointed Commandant of the Staff College, Camberley.   On the 14th all Officers attended at Divisional Headquarters to say good-bye to Major-General Sir Hugh Jeudwine, K.C.B., the Divisional Commander, on his

departure to command the Lancashire Division of
the Army of Occupation on the Rhine. Sir Hugh
also made a tour of the Division and said good-bye to
as many as possible of the rank and file.

Finally, the Cadre Party of the Battalion, composed
of Lieut.-Colonel R. Gardner, M.C., Lieut. T. H.
Pritchard, M.C., Lieut. R. W. Higginson, M.C., and
Captain P. W. Powell, M.C., the Quarter-Master,
and 24 Other Ranks, left Brussels early on Saturday
morning, June 7th, for England. They arrived at
Ulverston on Wednesday, June 11th, and were met
at the station by the Battalion Band, under Band-
master F. W. Garnett, and an enthusiastic concourse
of the population. On the following day there was a
Civic ceremony of welcome to the returning troops.
This was attended by Lieut.-Colonel W. F. A.
Wadham, V.D., Colonel G. H. Huthwaite, V.D.,
Major N. E. Barnes, T.D., Captain R. H. Horne, and
Captain J. Rawlinson, of the late Volunteers. Speeches
of welcome were made by Councillor C. J. Chapman
of the Ulverston Urban District Council, and Alderman
Mawson and Alderman Bradshaw, of the Barrow
Municipal Council. A procession was then formed to
the Ulverston Parish Church, and the Colours, carried
by Lieuts. Pritchard and Higginson, were deposited
for safe custody in the hands of the Rector, the Rev.
J. Stuart Rimmer, M.A. The Cadre Party then
re-formed, and marched back to the Drill Hall, where
some of them had mobilized nearly five years
previously—an event which seemed to belong to a
period incredibly remote.

J. CROSSLEY, *Captain,*

Late 1/4 *King's Own Royal Regiment.*

ULVERSTON,
     July, 1935.

APPENDIX " A."

4th Battalion
The King's Own (Royal Lancaster Regiment).

✧ ✧ ✧

Nominal Roll of Officers Mobilized with the Battalion, 4th August, 1914.

✧ ✧ ✧

Lieut. Colonel...   W. F. A. WADHAM, V.D., Commanding.

Majors   ...   ...   E. B. POOLEY.
R. THOMPSON.

Captains ...   ...   N. E. BARNES.
G. D. WADHAM.
R. P. LITTLE.
J. CADDY.
W. D. BARRATT.
W. G. PEARSON.
J. V. BARROW.

Lieutenants   ...   D. L. McNAUGHTAN.
G. B. BALFOUR.
J. S. FOTHERGILL.
R. D. MORRELL.
J. M. MAWSON.
W. H. B. R. KENNEDY.

2nd Lieutenants   H. Y. HUTHWAITE.
A. BEARDSLEY.
JOHN FISHER.
G. H. WALKER.

Adjutant...   ...   V. A. JACKSON, Captain (York and Lancaster Regt.).

Medical Officer   A. F. RUTHERFORD, Major, R.A.M.C. (T.F.).

I

APPENDIX "B."

4th Battalion
The King's Own (Royal Lancaster Regiment).

❖ ❖ ❖

Nominal Roll of Officers who Proceeded Overseas, 3rd May, 1915.

❖ ❖ ❖

Lieut. Colonel...   W. F. A. WADHAM, V.D., Commanding.

Majors ... ...   R. THOMPSON.
              N. E. BARNES.

Captains ... ...   R. P. LITTLE.
              J. CADDY.
              W. D. BARRATT.
              W. G. PEARSON.
              J. V. BARROW.
              G. B. BALFOUR.
              R. D. MORRELL (killed in action).
              J. M. MAWSON.

Lieutenants ...   G. H. WALKER (killed in action).
              H. Y. HUTHWAITE.
              A. BEARDSLEY.
              JOHN FISHER.
              E. H. HEWITT (killed in action).
              R. GARDNER.
              G. F. TAYLOR.
              A. A. WRIGHT (killed in action).

2nd Lieutenants   E. TILLYARD.
              W. C. NEILL.
              E. SPEARING (killed in action).
              G. B. BIGLAND (killed in action).
              H. A. BROCKLEBANK.
              H. R. SYKES.
              T. W. DUGDALE.
              JAMES FISHER.

Adjutant... ...   V. A. JACKSON, Captain (York and Lancaster Regt.).

Quartermaster   J. CROSSLEY, Lieutenant.

Medical Officer   A. F. RUTHERFORD, Major, R.A.M.C. (T.F.).

APPENDIX " C."

Additional Nominal Roll of Officers who served with the 1/4th Battalion The King's Own Royal Regt. (in order of joining) :—

Lieut. B. A. Leslie
2nd Lt. H. H. Hodgkinson
„ C. G. Chapman
„ G. J. Purnell
„ E. D. M. Meyler
„ H. Peak.
„ J. Finlay.
„ F. W. E. Keller
„ J. Ward
Lt. Col. F. M. Carleton, D.S.O.
2nd Lt. R. L. Purnell
Lieut. J. A. T. Clarke
2nd Lt. L. Bowman
„ P. J. Blundell
„ D. Dugdale
„ J. S. Corless
„ E. Myatt
„ J. Welch
„ W. B. McCall
Lieut. T. W. Dugdale
2nd Lt. C. Thorpe
„ Jas. Fisher
„ G. H. Ferns
„ C. E. Withey
„ J. D. Johnstone
„ E. E. McClinton
„ S. Steeples
„ O. R. Lees
„ G. R. Glenie
„ A. M. Clarke
„ G. Hilton
„ S. G. Voyle
„ S. F. Walker
„ J. Jackson
„ R. G. Metcalf
„ A. J. Brockman
„ J. M. Wilcock
„ L. Metcalfe
„ J. R. Lawson
Lt. Col. J. L. Swainson, D.S.O.
2nd Lt. H. H. Counsell
„ J. J. Rudduck
„ C. E. Lincey
„ R. W. Higginson
„ R. Bradley
„ S. Bolton
„ J. S. Ridsdale
„ H. V. Johnstone
„ E. D. Howard

2nd Lt. C. G. Lingford
„ R. Rule
„ H. V. R. T. Lauder
„ C. F. R. Crawshaw
„ J. D. Johnson
„ R. C. Hallam
„ T. F. Beasley
„ A. B. Park
„ A. P. Procter
„ F. J. Smith
„ A. Ellwood
„ B. J. H. Garnett
„ P. C. Taylor
„ H. O. Coleman
Capt. F. Williamson
„ F. C. Slater
Lieut. W. R. Pattinson
„ G. Topham
„ J. H. Simpson
2nd Lt. R. A. Mudie
„ A. T. Sheahan
„ R. Willett
„ J. Pearson
„ C. J. Alexander
„ J. S. Paterson
„ C. W. Ford
„ R. Holdsworth
„ H. A. Kershaw
„ R. G. Hatcher
„ J. H. Evans
„ J. A. McGill
„ A. E. Morton
„ C. H. Newbold
„ R. J. Warbrick
Major P. E. Robathan
2nd Lt. J. Thompson
„ R. M. Senton
„ H. G. R. Scaife
„ C. W. Gribble
„ D. G. Pearson
„ G. A. Taylor
„ A. S. Latham
„ W. Ratock
„ H. R. Hart
„ J. R. Gaulter
Lt. & Q.M. P. W. Powell
2nd Lt. F. C. Gilling
„ W. E. Jones
„ J. Way
„ T. H. Middleton

2nd Lt. E. T. White
„ E. S. Veevers
„ E. Haslam
„ N. Whittaker
„ T. H. C. Pritchard
Capt. T. N. Blain
2nd Lt. A. Binnie
„ F. J. Shuker
„ B. Gough
„ L. R. Keighley
„ N. Walkden
„ J. R. Rundle
„ A. J. Thorpe
„ W. McAndrew
„ J. McKay
„ B. H. Pemberton
„ N. F. Paterson
„ G. N. Russell
„ G. F. Raeside
„ H. G. Rowe
„ J. H. Sykes
„ R. Smith
„ W. Stewart
„ A. J. Dartnall
„ R. S. Dane
„ G. Field
„ R. W. Higginson
„ G. W. Ferguson
„ C. J. Holland
„ M. Smith
„ J. H. Collin
„ A. Thomson
„ L. F. Fouraker
„ H. Hunter
„ S. Bolton
„ J. H. Hamer
„ J. G. Anderson
„ R. A. Taylor
„ A. Fyfe
„ T. S. Paterson
Capt. E. A. Kendall
„ C. L. Overton, M.C.
„ J. I. Simpson, M.C.
2nd Lt. W. J. Holmes, M.C.
„ A. W. Wyncoll
„ H. J. Lyon
„ E. Willis
„ T. C. Threadgold
„ H. W. T. Chalcraft

2nd Lt. R. Court
  ,, G. A. K. Islip
  ,, L. R. Andrews
  ,, I. B. Rouse
  ,, G. M. Gray
  ,, H. Barrow
  ,, D. B. Shutt
Lieut. H. S. Brown

2nd Lt. G. Ribchester
  ,, E. D. Osgood
  ,, D. O. Maclean
           M.C.
  ,, A. Whitmore
Capt. W. K. Batchelor
2nd Lt. C. A. Russell
Capt. B. Peers

Lieut. R. L. Ashcroft
  ,, E. H. T. Tucker
  ,, A. H. Tollemache
2nd Lt. A. C. Notley
  ,, G. H. Lowery
  ,, H. E. Godfrey
  ,, J. A. Vincent
Lieut. W. L. Rudall
2nd Lt. N. R. Hutley
  ,, L. E. Wharton
  ,, T. D. R. Crilly
  ,, F. C. Place, M.M.
  ,, F. C. Waywell
  ,, H. Richardson,
           D.C.M.
  ,, R. H. Robinson
  ,, G. W. E. . Sanderson

2nd Lt. W. Shaw
  ,, J. A. Thomas
  ,, E. Williams
  ,, J. Grindal
  ,, W. Y. Gleave
  ,, J. J. R. Larkin
  ,, J. G. Anderson
  ,, E. Lockey
  ,, A. W. Rigg
  ,, D. Burr
  ,, H. S. Scott
  ,, J. W. Lugard
  ,, S. Smith
Lieut. A. Fraser
Capt. R. T. Bethune
2nd Lt. J. B. Lindsay
  ,, C. Elliott

DEPARTMENTAL OFFICERS ATTACHED.

Capt. J. S. Titmas,
      R.A.M.C.
Lieut. J. H. C. Gatchell,
      R.A.M.C.

Capt. J. S. G. Wilson,
      R.A.M.C.
Rev. R. H. Hingley, C.F.

Rev. R. Gillenders, C.F.
Rev. T. L. B. Westerdale,
      C.F.

APPENDIX " D."

OFFICERS' CASUALTIES.

KILLED IN ACTION.

2nd Lt. G. B. Bigland
Lieut. S. Bolton
2nd Lt. L. Bowman,
      R.A.F.
  ,, R. Bradley
  ,, A. J. Brockman
Lieut. A. M. Clark
2nd Lt. J. H. Collin
  ,, R. Court
  ,, A. J. Dartnall
  ,, T. W. Dugdale
Capt. A. Ellwood
2nd Lt. C. W. Ford
  ,, G. R. Glenie
  ,, B. H. Gough

Lieut. E. H. Hewitt

2nd Lt. G. Hilton
  ,, H. H. Hodgkinson
  ,, C. J. Holland
  ,, E. D. Howard
  ,, H. Hunter
  ,, J. D. Johnstone
  ,, P. Jolly
  ,, J. P. Lawson
  ,, W. R. Leah
  ,, C. E. Lincey
  ,, L. Metcalf

Capt. R. D. A. Morrell

2nd Lt. A. C. Notley
  ,, F. C. Place
  ,, G. F. Raeside
  ,, B. H. Robinson
  ,, J. R. Rundle
Lieut. E. Scott-Miller
  ,, E. Spearing
2nd Lt. A. Thomson
  ,, E. S. Veevers
Lieut. G. H. Walker
2nd Lt. E. T. White
Capt. C. E. Withey
  ,, A. A. Wright

DIED OF WOUNDS.

2nd Lt. R. G. Hatcher
  ,, L. R. Keighley
Lieut. J. J. Rudduck

Lt. Col. J. L. Swainson,
      D.S.O.
2nd Lt. A. Wheatley

2nd Lt. J. Ward
     (accidentally)

WOUNDED IN ACTION.

2nd Lt. J. C. Alexander
  ,,   J. G. Anderson
  ,,   J. W. H. Axtell
  ,,   F. F. Beazley
Capt. T. R. Blain
  ,,   H. A. Brocklebank
2nd Lt. L. Bowman
  ,,   A. M. Clarke
Capt. J. A. T. Clarke
2nd Lt. H. H. Counsell
  ,,   G. F. H.
            Crawshaw
  ,,   W. Eatock
  ,,   G. W. Ferguson
  ,,   G. H. Ferns
  ,,   G. Field
Lieut. R. Gardner
      (accidentally)
2nd Lt. J. R. Gaulter
  ,,   F. C. Gilling
  ,,   J. Grindal
  ,,   R. C. Hallam
  ,,   H. R. Hart
  ,,   E. Haslam
  ,,   J. D. Johnstone

Capt. F. Jones
2nd Lt. W. E. Jones
  ,,   L. R. Keighley
  ,,   J. J. R. Larkin
  ,,   C. G. Lingford
  ,,   J. Mackay
  ,,   J. A. McGill
  ,,   R. G. Metcalfe
  ,,   T. H. Middleton
Capt. W. C. Neill
2nd Lt. C. H. Newbold
Capt. W. R. Pattinson
2nd Lt. B. H. Pemberton
  ,,   R. L. Purnell
  ,,   A. W. Rigg
  ,,   I. B. Rouse
  ,,   J. J. Rudduck
  ,,   G. W. E.
            Sanderson
  ,,   H. G. Scaife
  ,,   R. M. Senton
  ,,   W. Shaw
  ,,   F. J. Smith
  ,,   N. Smith
  ,,   R. Smith

Lieut. E. Spearing
2nd Lt. S. Steeple
  ,,   W. McK. Stewart
  ,,   H. R. Sykes
  ,,   J. H. Sykes
  ,,   G. A. Taylor
  ,,   P. C. Taylor
  ,,   J. Thompson
Lt. Col. R. Thompson
2nd Lt. A. J. Thorpe
  ,,   A. Turner
  ,,   S. G. Voyle
      (accidentally)
  ,,   N. Walkden
  ,,   S. F. Walker
  ,,   H. J. Warbrick
  ,,   F. C. Waywell
  ,,   H. Welsh
  ,,   L. E. Wharton
  ,,   A. Whitmore
  ,,   N. Whittaker
  ,,   J. M. Wilcock
Capt. F. H. Williamson
2nd Lt. C. E. Withey

MISSING.

2nd Lt. W. Holmes (and
      wounded)
Lieut. A. S. Latham

2nd Lt. W. McAndrews
  ,,   E. D. Osgood
  ,,   R. Smith

2nd Lt. R. A. Taylor
  ,,   T. C. Threadgold

PRISONERS OF WAR.

2nd Lt. G. Field   Capt. W. G. Pearson (and wounded)

AWARDS.

VICTORIA CROSS.

2nd Lieut. J. H. Collin (Posthumous)

DISTINGUISHED SERVICE ORDER (and Bar).

Lt. Col. G. B. Balfour

MILITARY CROSS.

2nd Lt. J. C. Alexander
  ,,   L. R. Andrews
  ,,   T. S. Bateson
Capt. T. R. Blain
2nd Lt. R. S. Dane
Capt. A. Ellwood
  ,,   J. H. Evans
  ,,   R. Gardner

2nd Lt. J. R. Gaulter
Capt. H. Y. Huthwaite
  ,,   E. A. Kendall
2nd Lt. A. S. Latham
Capt. A. E. Morton
2nd Lt. B. H. Pemberton
  ,,   F. C. Place, M.M.
Lieut. P. W. Powell

2nd Lt. T. H. Pritchard
Capt. A. P. Procter
2nd Lt. G. F. Raeside
  ,,   H. Richardson
  ,,   I. B. Rouse
  ,,   G. A. Taylor
Capt. A. A. Wright

FRENCH CROIX-DE-GUERRE.

Capt. J. A. T. Clarke   2nd Lt. R. C. Hallam

MENTIONED IN DESPATCHES.

Lt. Col. G. B. Balfour   2nd Lt. H. R. Hart   Lieut. G. F. Taylor
(three times)   Lieut. E. H. Hewitt   „   E. Myatt

BROUGHT TO THE NOTICE OF THE SECRETARY OF STATE "FOR VALUABLE SERVICES RENDERED IN CONNECTION WITH THE WAR."

Lt. Col. W. F. A. Wadham, V.D.

APPENDIX "E."
RANK AND FILE.
KILLED IN ACTION.

Pte. T. H. Agar
„ T. Airey
L/Cpl. T. Akister
Pte. R. Allen
„ T. Angrove
„ G. Ashcroft
„ G. Ashworth
„ A. Askew
„ H. R. Atkinson
„ J. Atkinson
„ T. Bagot
„ H. Bailey
Cpl. T. Balderston
Pte. J. J. Barrow
„ E. Baxendale
„ T. Baxter
„ W. Beckitt
„ W. Bell
„ F. Bellamy
L/Cpl. J. Bennett
Pte. J. Bennett
„ H. Bland
„ T. Bowron
„ J. Brack
L/Cpl. R. W. Bransden
Pte. V. Brazil
L/Cpl. W. T. Brew
L/Sgt. J. Brocklebank
Pte. J. J. Brocklebank
„ P. Brogan
L/Cpl. J. A. Brookes
„ J. Brown
Pte. L. E. Burley
Sgt. F. J. Burn
Pte. M. Burton

L/Sgt. M. Caddy
Pte. F. Carson
„ R. Carter
„ S. Carter
„ J. Cartwright
„ E. Catterall
„ A. Chadwick
Sgt. J. Charnock
Pte. H. Churm
„ J. Cloudsdale
„ E. Coles
„ J. Collier
„ T. E. Collinge
L/Cpl. J. Collinson
Pte. J. Cooley
„ S. Corbett
„ W. Cottam
„ A. Coulter
„ B. Crispe
„ W. Croasdale
Sgt. J. M. Cross
Pte. T. Crossman
„ H. Currie
„ E. Curwen
„ C. Davies
„ W. Dean
L/Cpl. A. Diggle
Pte. R. Dixon
„ H. Dobson
„ J. Dodd
„ R. Donovan
„ A. Downham
„ W. A. Downham
„ J. Duckworth
„ P. Duerden

Sgt. S. Eagers
Pte. T. Eccles
L/Cpl. T. Else
Pte. F. Elston
„ H. Evans
„ E. Fairhurst
„ W. T. A. Fell
„ E. Fisher
„ J. Fitzwilliam
Sgt. G. Fletcher
Pte. F. J. Fletcher
„ T. Ford
„ J. H. Frawley
„ H. Fryer
„ C. Gawne
„ W. Gentles
„ J. E. Gill
„ W. Glover
„ J. Green
„ J. Greenhalgh
„ E. Grey
„ J. Griffiths
„ E. Hadwin
„ E. Hall
„ G. Hardcastle
„ J. Hargreaves
L/Cpl. J. E. Haslam
Pte. W. Haythorn
„ E. Haythornwaite
„ H. Hayward
„ J. Hems
„ T. Hesketh
„ L. Higgs
„ J. Hilton
„ T. Hodgson

Pte. W. C. Hogg
,, J. Hoggarth
,, H. Hoole
,, R. Houghton
,, P. Howcroft
,, R. Hughes
L/Sgt. W. S. Inman
Cpl. T. Jackson
Pte. T. James
,, W. Jameson
L/Cpl. N. Jamieson
,, J. Jarvis
Pte. J. Johnson
,, J. Johnson
,, P. Johnson
,, W. E. Johnson
,, R. L. Jones
,, J. T. Kay
,, A. Kelly
,, W. Knipe
,, R. Knowles
,, A. Lancaster
,, D. Leach
,, E. Lenanghan
Cpl. N. Lewis
Pte. W. Liptrot
,, J. W. Lister
,, J. E. Lock
L/Cpl. J. Lockhead
Pte. T. Lofthouse
Cpl. T. Long
Pte. W. Long
,, L. Longworth
,, R. Lovell
L/Cpl. T. A. Lowe
Pte. D. Maler
,, H. Mason
,, W. Mason
Cpl. W. Masters
Pte. J. Mather
L/Sgt. J. H. Mellon
Pte. G. Mercer
Sgt. J. Miles
Pte. J. Miles
,, J. Millington
Cpl. W. H. Milton
Pte. J. Mitchell
,, E. V. Monks
,, W. Moran
,, G. Moses
,, S. Myerscough
,, J. McAlarney
,, A. McDowell
,, J. H. McGill

Pte. J. H. McGowan
,, W. J. McKay
,, J. McQuade
,, B. McVittie
,, R. H. Nelson
,, J. E. S. Newby
,, E. Nicholson
L/Cpl. J. J. Nicholson
Pte. J. Nightingale
,, R. Noble
,, A. Nuttall
,, J. Nutter
,, S. Oliver
L/Cpl. W. O'Neill
,, R. Oversby
C.Q.M.S. Page
Pte. H. Parker
,, J. J. Parsons
,, R. Penaluna
,, J. H. Perry
Cpl. J. W. Pettitt
Pte. C. S. Petty
L/Sgt. H. H. Pill
Pte. W. R. Pimm
,, C. Pittaway
Cpl. J. Postlethwaite
Pte. R. F. Postlethwaite
,, W. Postlethwaite
,, J. Powell
,, H. Pownall
Cpl. R. Proudfoot
Pte. J. Ratcliffe
Sgt. T. S. Rathbone
Pte. T. Raven
,, W. Rawsthorne
Sgt. J. Reid
Pte. H. Ribiero
Cpl. S. Richardson
Pte. F. P. Rigg
Sgt. G. Robinson
,, R. Robinson
L/Cpl. S. Robinson
Pte. W. Robinson
Cpl. D. G. Rowlandson
Pte. J. Royle
L/Cpl. F. Ryder
Pte. E. Salthouse
L/Cpl. J. Sandilands
Pte. J. E. Scargill
,, E. Sellars
,, C. Settle
,, A. Sharp
,, T. Sharp

L/Sgt. C. Shaw
Pte. R. Shaw
L/Cpl. F. Shepherd
Pte. R. Shone
,, A. Sidebottom
,, G. Simpson
,, G. Simpson
Cpl. A. Singleton
Pte. J. A. Singleton
,, H. E. Slaymaker
,, F. Smith
L/Cpl. P. Smith
Pte. P. Stanworth
Sgt. R. L. Steel
Pte. A. F. Stevens
Cpl. W. Stewart
Pte. J. Strickland
,, F. Swainson
,, C. Swift
,, J. Swindlehurst
,, W. Sykes
,, J. W. Taylor
,, H. Thompson
Sgt. R. Thompson
Pte. W. Thompson
,, G. Titterington
Sgt. R. E. Titterington
Pte. L. Truran
,, F. Twynham
,, G. F. Tyer
,, L. Tyson
,, R. Tyson
,, W. Unsworth
Sgt. R. Usher
L/Cpl. D. Vickers
Pte. J. Vincent
,, H. D. Vity
,, L. Wade
,, J. Walker
,, J. Walmsley
,, R. M. Walters
Sgt. G. H. Watson
Pte. J. T. Watts
,, F. Webster
,, J. Whiteway
,, T. Whittle
,, J. Wild
Sgt. J. Williams
Pte. W. Williams
L/Cpl. J. Wilson
Pte. J. Winder
L/Cpl. R. Woodward
Pte. J. Young

DIED OF WOUNDS.

Pte. R. Abbott
L/Sergt. C. E. Ansell
Pte. T. Ashton

Pte. J. Atherton
,, A. Baker
,, H. E. Barker

Pte. S. Barnett
,, W. H. Barrow
L/Cpl. J. Barry

Cpl. F. Baxter
Pte. J. Benson
,, W. Bevins
,, J. Bowfield
,, E. M. Burne
Sgt. F. Cannon
Pte. W. Carradus
,, E. J. Carton
,, J. B. Clayton
,, J. Coombe
,, J. Cooper
,, R. Corlett
,, C. Cragg
,, W. Crossland
,, J. Dyson
,, C. R. Eastham
,, T. Eccles
,, A. Evans
,, R. E. Fenton
Cpl. W. M. Fletcher
Pte. J. Fortune
,, T. Fox
,, A. H. Garnett
,, S. Geldart
C.S.M. H. P. Gendle
Pte. C. Gregory
,, F. Griffies
,, H. Hadfield
,, W. Harrison
,, P. Higson

L/Sgt. H. Hinchcliffe
Pte. W. R. Holmes
,, J. Hoole
,, W. Hutton
,, J. Kelly
,, J. T. King
,, W. Lawson
,, W. Mathews
,, G. A. Merritt
,, R. H. A. Moreton
L/Sgt. C. Morris
Pte. D. Muncaster
L/Cpl. N. McKenzie
Pte. J. McMahon
Cpl. H. Neal
Pte. M. Newby
,, W. Nicholson
,, T. E. Noble
L/Cpl. J. Oxley
Pte. G. E. Park
,, W. Penny
,, W. Phillips
L/Cpl. R. Porter
Pte. G. Poskitt
,, T. Preston
Sgt. J. H. Quayle
,, A. Redman
L/Col. J. Riley
Pte. G. W. Robinson
,, B. Rogerson

Pte. F. Rothersay
,, W. Rowlands
,, W. R. Rowlands
,, H. W. Rudge
,, G. W. Rylands
,, H. Simmons
,, W. Smedley
,, H. Smith
,, A. Solari
,, J. Sprout
,, H. Stott
,, H. Symons
,, F. Talbot
Sgt. L. C. Taylor
Pte. J. Topping
L/Cpl. H. Q. Towers
Pte. W. G. Trewern
,, T. C. Vargoe
,, R. Wallace
,, E. Watson
,, J. Whalley
,, T. Wharton
,, T. Whiteside
,, T. Whiting
,, J. Whittam
,, J. Whittam
,, J. Wilding
,, H. Wilson
,, W. Wooff
,, F. H. Worth

APPENDIX " F."

RANK AND FILE.

WOUNDED IN ACTION.

Pte. W. Abernethy
,, J. Abram
,, A. Akred
,, W. Allen
,, R. Anderton
,, T. Angrove
L/Cpl. L. Andrewartha
Pte. R. J. Armstrong
,, A. Arnold
,, W. G. Arnott
,, R. Ashburner
,, T. Ashburner
,, G. Ashcroft
,, H. T. Ashnore
,, J. Ashnore
,, T. Ashton
L/Cpl. J. Ashworth
Pte. Aspinall
,, J. Astley
,, J. Atherton
,, J. Atkinson
,, J. Atkinson

Pte. J. J. Atkinson
L/Sgt. Atkinson
Pte. T. Atkinson
,, H. Backhouse
,, J. Backhouse
,, T. Baker
,, A. Bagshaw
,, J. Bailey
,, P. Bailey
,, R. Balderson
Cpl. J. Balderston
Pte. A. Baldwin
,, T. Balm
L/Cpl. H. Bamber
Pte. J. Bamber
,, J. R. Bamber
,, H. E. Barker
,, W. Barker
,, G. Barnes
,, S. Barnett
Cpl. E. W. Barrow
Pte. F. Barrow

Pte. W. Barrow
,, P. Barton
L/Sgt. C. Bates
Pte. H. Bebbington
,, H. Back
,, R. Bee
Cpl. R. Bell
C.S.M. W. Bell
Cpl. E. Bennett
Pte. N. Bennett
,, R. J. Bennett
,, S. Bennett
,, T. Benson
,, D. Berwick
,, T. Beswick
,, E. Bevins
,, T. E. Bewsher
,, T. H. Bewsher
,, H. Bidwell
,, A. V. Billington
,, T. Binns
,, C. E. Birch

Pte. R. Birkett
„ E. Birmingham
„ D. Black
L/Cpl. J. Blake
„ W. Blackburn
Pte. W. Blakeborough
„ E. Blamire
„ S. Bloomfield
„ G. Bool
„ W. Boom
„ T. Bowers
„ J. Bowling
„ G. Bowman
„ J. Boylan
L/Cpl. H. Bradley
Pte. A. Brady
„ J. Braithwaite
C.S.M. T. Braithwaite
Pte. W. Braithwaite
„ R. Brannon
L/Sgt. R. Bray
„ W. Bray
Pte. H. Brewer
Sgt. J. Brewer
Pte. H. Bridge
„ C. Brocklebank
„ J. T. Brocklebank
„ W. Brocklebank
„ G. Broderick
„ R. Brookes
Sgt. C. Brown
Pte. R. Brown
„ G. W. Brunskill
L/Cpl. D. Bryan
Pte. J. Bulderson
„ N. Bullivant
„ J. T. Bullock
„ J. Bumford
(accidentally)
„ T. Bunford
„ E. Burley
„ H. Burley
Sgt. J. F. Burns
Cpl. J. Burns
Pte. E. N. Burns
„ F. Burns
„ J. J. Burns
„ J. W. Burns
„ J. Burrows
Sgt. A. Burton
C.S.M. R. Butcher
L/Cpl. H. Butler
Pte. G. W. Caine
„ V. Cairns
„ R. Campbell
„ W. Canning
„ J. Cannon
„ J. Capstick
„ J. Cardwell
„ J. Carrick

Sgt. J. Carrick
Pte. R. Carter
„ T. Carter
„ E. J. Cartwright
Cpl. J. H. Casper
Pte. F. Casson
Sgt. T. J. Chapple
Pte. H. Chadderton
„ I. Chadwick
„ T. Chadwick
Sgt. W. Chadwick
Pte. W. J. Chapman
Sgt. J. Charnock
Pte. J. T. Charters
Sgt. T. W. Cheeseman
Pte. L. Chorlton
„ W. P. Christian
„ S. Christie
Sgt. F. Clampitt
Pte. J. Clare
„ W. Clare
L/Cpl. A. Clark
Cpl. G. Clarke
Pte. J. H. Clarke
„ J. Clarke
„ R. Clarke
„ S. Clarke
„ W. Clarke
„ E. Clarkson
„ J. B. Clayton
„ R. Clegg
„ A. Clemunson
„ W. Cooke
„ T. Connor
„ W. Conroy
„ T. Cooper
L/Cpl. C. Cooper
Pte. C. D. Corless
L/Cpl. E. Corbthwaite
Pte. J. Cottam
L/Cpl. J. Coultsman
Pts. S. Coupe
„ J. Coupland
L/Cpl. J. Coupland
Pte. H. G. Courtnell
Sgt. J. Coward
Pte. L. Coward
„ T. Coward
„ E. Cowell
Cpl. G. W. Cox
Pte. D. G. Craig
„ S. Crane
„ T. Cross
„ C. W. Crowther
„ J. E. Cuddy
„ M. Cunningham
„ H. Cunningham
„ R. Cunningham
„ J. Curran
„ W. G. Dacre

Pte. W. W. Dalton
„ H. Daly
„ W. Danson
„ S. Darby
„ F. Davies
„ H. Davies
„ J. Davies
„ G. Dawson
„ R. Dawson
L/Cpl. R. Dawson
Pte. M. Dembovski
„ E. M. Denny
„ W. H. Dent
„ H. Derbyshire
„ S. Derdle
„ J. E. Dewhurst
„ S. Dickinson
„ J. Dickson
„ A. Dixon
„ R. Dixon
„ S. Dixon
„ W. Dixon
„ J. Dobson
Sgt. G. Dockeray
Pte. G. H. Dowker
„ A. Downing
„ T. E. Drew
L/Cpl. M. Drinkall
Cpl. T. Dumphey
„ C. Durkin
Pte. J. Dyson
„ G. Eagers
(accidentally)
„ J. Eagle
„ J. W. Earnshaw
L/Sgt. H. Eastwood
Pte. E. Eaton
L/Cpl. G. Eddleston
Pte. A. Edge
„ F. Edmondson
L/Cpl. T. Edmondson
Pte. J. H. Edwards
„ E. Egan
„ J. Elcocks
„ T. Ellam
Cpl. T. Entwistle
L/Sgt. J. Erhart
Pte. W. Escolme
„ A. Evans
„ J. H. Evans
Sgt. W. H. Farish
Pte. R. Farnen
„ W. Farnworth
„ J. Farrell
„ R. Farrer
„ P. Fawcett
Cpl. T. Fawcett
Sgt. H. Fearnley
Pte. J. Fell (accidentally)
„ N. Fell

Pte. F. Fenwick
" W. Fisher
" H. Fitters
" T. Fitzsimmons
L/Cpl. W. Fitzsimmons
Pte. J. Fletcher
" J. W. Flitcroft
" S. Foster
" P. Fox
" W. France
L/Cpl. S. Friend
Pte. F. Froggart
" A. Fryer
" A. Fullard
" H. Fullard
" J. Fulwood
" J. Fury
" R. Gallagher
" J. R. Gardner
" J. Garner
" A. H. Garnett
" H. Garstang
" W. Garvey
" J. Gaskarth
C.S.M. H. P. Gendle
Pte. T. Gendle
" H. Gent
    (accidentally)
" W. Gilbert
" G. Gill
" A. Gillbanks
L/Cpl. H. Gildea
Pte. T. E. Gibbons
L/Cpl. H. Glaister
Pte. J. Glover
" W. Goldstan
" H. Gomersall
" J. Gooden
" H. Goodwin
" J. Goodwin
Sgt. F. L. Gott
Pte. S. J. Gowling
" F. Graham
" J. Greaves
" L. Gredy
" W. J. Green
" J. Greenhill
" A. Greenhow
" E. Greenhow
" H. Greenhow
" J. Greenhow
" J. Gregg
L/Sgt. J. Gregson
Pte. J. Grimshaw
" C. Grindrod
" H. Grisegale
" R. Grisedale
" G. Grosvenor
" A. Gunning
" H. R. Hackney

Pte. W. Hague
" S. A. Haines
" E. Hall
" J. Halsall
" J. W. Hamer
" F. Hampson
" W. Hampson
" F. Hanley
" T. Hargreaves
" J. Harris
" T. Harris
" H. Harrison
" J. Harrison
" J. R. Harrison
L/Cpl. R. Hartley
Pte. T. Haskett
" A Hawarden
" E. Hatchman
" W. J. Hawkins
" H. Haworth
" L. Healey
" H. Heaton
" G. Helme
" W. G. Helmsley
" R. Henderson
" T. Henderson
" R. Hesketh
" A. Hibbert
" C. Higginson
" T. H. High
" E. Hillen
Cpl. W. Hird
Pte. W. Hitchen
" R. Hodgson
L/Cpl. A. E. Hodgson
Pte. T. Hodgson
" W. Hodgson
L/Cpl. E. Hodgson
Pte. J. E. Hodgkinson
" J. Hogan
" J. Hoggarth
    (accidentally)
" J. Holgate
" J. Hollingworth
" A. Holman
L/Cpl. F. Holmes
" G. Holmes
Pte. W. M. Holmes
" W. L. Holroyd
C.S.M. R. H. Horne
Pte. H. Horrabin
" E. Hoskin(accidentally)
" J. Hoskin
Cpl. G. Hosking
Pte. E. J. Hoskins
" J. P. Hough
" T. Hovington
" F. Howarth
" G. Howarth
    (accidentally)

L/Cpl. T. Howarth
Pte. W. Howarth
L/Sgt. G. Huddleston
Pte. Huddleston
" J. R. Hughes
" R. A. Hughes
L/Cpl. S. Hughes
Pte. J. E. Hunt
" W. Hunter
" J. M. Hurst
" A. Hutchinson
L/Cpl. T. Hutchinson
Pte. S. Ibbotson
" C. Ingram
" R. W. Irving
" J. Irwin
" F. Isaacs
" A. Isherwood
L/Cpl. A. Jackson
Cpl. A. Jackson
L/Sgt. F. Jackson
Pte. H. Jackson
" S. Jackson
" W. Jackson
L/Cpl. W. H. Jackson
" W. W. Jackson
Sgt. W. W. Jackson
Pte. J. James
" T. James
L/Cpl. F. Jeffrey
Pte. W. J. Jeffrey
" W. Jenkinson
" J. H. Jervis
" J. Jines
" A. Johns
Pte. A. Johnson
" A. P. Johnson
" G. A. Johnson
Cpl. W. Johnston
Pte. C. Jones
" E. V. Jones
" F. Jones
" F. Kay
" A. Kay
" E. Keeton
Cpl. M. Keelan
L-Cpl. A. Kelly
Pte. E. Kelly
" J. Kelly
" P. R. Kemp
" J. Kempson
" J. Kendall
" W. Kewley
Sgt. W. Kirby
Pte. C. F. Kirkham
" H. Kinder
Cpl. H. H. Kitchen
Pte. J. Kitchen
Cpl. E. Kneebone
Pte. R. Knight

Pte. R. Lamb
L/Cpl. W. Lamb
Pte. F. Lanning
,, A. Lawrence
,, H. Lawrence
,, J. Lay
,, S. Leach
,, H. Leake
,, W. Leather
,, H. Lee
,, F. Lees
,, E. Lenenghan
,, W. Lever
,, A. Leviston
,, A. Lewis
,, R. Lewis
,, V. L. Lills
L/Cpl. J. Lingard
Pte. R. Littler
Cpl. W. Livesey
,, T. E. Lloyd
,, J. T. Loftus
Pte. J. Lomax
,, G. Long
Cpl. T. Long
Pte. W. E. Longcroft
,, C. Longworth
    (accidentally)
Cpl. O. Longworth
Pte. R. Lonsdale
,, J. Looms
,, J. E. Lowden
,, H. Lowe
,, J. Lowery
,, A. Lowther
,, W. Lucas
,, W. J. Lunt
,, F. Mackintosh
Sgt. W. Maden
Pte. E. W. Magor
,, T. Makinson
,, M. Mannion
,, W. Marland
Pte. C. Marr
,, S. Marr
,, J. W. Marshall
,, H. Marshall
,, W. Marshall
Cpl. H. Martin
Pte. T. H. Martin
,, J. Martindale
,, T. Martindale
,, F. Mason
,, W. Mason
,, A. Mawson
Cpl. T. Mayson
Pte. J. Meikleham
,, J. Melia
,, G. Melling
L/Cpl. J. Mellor

Pte. J. I. Menzies
,, R. Mercer
,, R. Merrett
Sgt. T. H. Middleton
Pte. D. Miller
,, F. H. Miller
L/Cpl. W. Miller
Pte. G. Millett
,, A. S. Milligan
,, G. Milligan
,, J. Millington
,, A. Mills
,, J. B. Mitchell
L/Sgt. R. Mollard
Pte. R. Monks
,, W. Monks
,, B. Moore
,, R. Moorhouse
,, J. Moreland
,, J. Morgan
,, S. Morgan
Sgt. J. P. Morgan
L/Cpl. A. S. Morris
Pte. A. Morrow
,, R. Morton
,, L. Mountcastle
,, J. Murphy
,, P. J. Murphy
,, J. P. Murphy
,, J. Murray
,, W. Mylchreest
,, A. McBride
    (accidentally)
,, A. McVaig
,, R. McDonald
,, B. McGuinness
,, A. McKenzie
,, F. McKeown
,, R. McKeron
,, A. McLaughlin
,, D. McLaughlin
,, J. McMahon
,, J. McMasters
,, S. McNa
,, P. McPoland
L/Cpl. A. McWilliams
Pte. L. Nazelcop
,, J. Neild
,, S. Nelson
,, R. E. Newby
,, T. H. Newby
Sgt. E. L. Newham
Pte. F. J. Newling
Sgt. E. Newton
Pte. J. Newton
,, F. R. Nicholas
,, J. Nicholls
,, C. Nickolas
,, W. Nickolas
L/Cpl. H. Nightingale

Pte. D. F. Noake
,, T. E. Noble
,, H. Nock
,, F. H. Nolan
,, J. Notman
,, J. Nottle
,, J. H. Nunn
,, S. Nuttall
,, T. O'Brien
,, G. D. Ogden
,, G. R. Outham
,, W. J. Orton
,, E. Osborne
,, W. H. Paine
,, H. A. Palethorpe
,, J. T. Palmer
,, N. Palmer
,, F. Parker
,, G. H. Parker
,, J. E. Parker
,, W. Parker
,, W. H. Parker
,, A. W. Parkinson
,, T. Parkinson
,, W. Parkinson
,, W. T. Parkinson
Sgt. H. Parnell
L/Cpl. J. S. Parry
Pte. T. A. Parsons
,, M. H. Patterson
,, J. Pattinson
,, J. C. Peake
,, E. Pearson
L/Sgt. F. Pearson
Sgt. J. R. Pearson
Pte. H. Perceval
L/Cpl. H. Phillips
Pte. J. Phillips
,, A. Phizacklea
,, E. Phizacklea
Sgt. R. W. Pickin
Pte. W. Pickles
,, F. Pickthall
    (accidentally)
,, J. Pierson
,, A. Pilkington
,, J. Pilkington
,, A. Pill
,, R. Pipe
,, W. Pinch
,, J. H. Platt
,, J. Pollitt
,, J. Porter
,, J. W. Porter
Cpl. M. J. Porter
Pte. J. Postlethwaite
,, J. Preston
,, T. Preston
,, D. Preston
,, C. J. Price

Pte. H. Price
,, A. Priestley
,, J. Pritchard
,, R. Proctor
,, H. Proudfoot
,, T. Purcell
L/Cpl. J. Purviss
Pte. A. B. Pyle
Dr. G. Quigley
Pte. P. Quinn
,, G. Radford
,, J. Rafferty
,, H. Railton
,, J. Ralph
,, J. Ramsbottom
,, W. Ranger
,, H. Ratcliffe
,, G. J. Rawlinson
,, G. Read
,, W. Reddicliffe
Sgt. A. Redman
Cpl. S. W. Redman
Pte. J. Reeve
,, T. Rennison
,, E. Retallick
,, A. Rhodes
Sgt. F. Richardson
Pte. S. Richardson
,, C. Riddle
,, H. Riding
,, W. Ridings
,, T. E. Ridley
,, H. Rigg
    (accidentally)
,, H. Rimmer
,, J. Roberts
,, W. J. Roberts
Sgt. F. Robertson
Pte. E. Robinson
,, E. G. Robinson
,, W. Robinson
,, F. Robson
,, W. Rockcliffe
,, J. Rogerson
,, W. Roebuck
,, A. Rollinson
L/Cpl. G. Rorison
Pte. R. Rorison
,, F. Rose
,, S. V. Rose
Cpl. T. Rose
Pte. J. Round
,, A. Rowe
,, S. Rowe
,, S. J. Rowe
,, A. Rusconi
,, F. Rush
,, W. Rushton
,, G. W. Rylands
,, H. Sadler

Pte. J. Sanderson
,, J. Sandilands
,, F. W. Sarrett
,, A. Saunders
,, F. W. Saunders
Cpl. E. Savage
Pte. J. Savage
,, E. Scall
,, W. Schofield
,, J. Scholes
,, W. Scott
Pte. T. Scrogham
,, W. Scrogham
,, J. Sharples
L/Cpl. H. Shaw
Pte. H. Shaw
,, L. Shaw
L/Sgt. H. Shelley
Pte. B. Shepherd
L/Cpl. J. T. Shepherd
Pte. T. Shepherd
,, R. Simm
L/Cpl. G. Simpson
Pte. R. Simpson
,, S. Simpson
,, P. Singleton
,, E. Slater
Cpl. R. Slater
Pte. W. Slater
,, J. E. Slinger
,, T. Small
,, B. Smith
,, G. Smith
,, Jas. Smith
    (accidentally)
,, J. Smith
,, J. Smith
L/Sgt. J. Smith
Cpl. J. D. Smith
Pte. H. Smith
,, N. Smith
,, T. Smith
,, W. Smith
L/Cpl. W. H. Smith
Pte. J. D. Speakman
,, S. Spencer
,, L. Springthorpe
,, G. Sprout
,, H. Sprout
,, J. Sprout
,, T. Stables
,, J. Steel
L/Cpl. W. Steel
Pte. F. Steele
,, W. Steele
,, J. Stenchion
,, L. G. Stephens
L/Cpl. E. Stephenson
Pte. J. Stephenson
,, W. Stevens

Pte. C. Stewart
,, R. Stirrup
,, W. Stone
Cpl. C. D. Stops
Pte. F. Storey
,, H. Stott
,, B. Stowe
,, G. Strickland
,, W. Summerson
,, L. Swainson
C.S.M. A. Sweeney
Pte. D. Talbot
L/Cpl. A. V. Taylor
,, J. Taylor
Sgt. L. C. Taylor
Pte. M. Taylor
,, T. Taylor
,, W. W. Taylor
,, A. Tennant
,, R. Terry
,, G. F. Tevevdale
,, E. E. Thomas
Pte. A. Thompson
,, F. Thompson
,, G. T. Thompson
,, J. G. Thompson
L/Cpl. J. H. Thompson
Pte. R. Thompson
,, R. S. Thompson
,, W. W. Thompson
Cpl. W. Thompson
Pte. W. Thompson
,, F. T. Thorley
,, J. M. Thornley
,, W. Thornborough
Sgt. F. J. Threblecock
Pte. W. Threlfall
,, J. H. Tildesley
,, W. Tindall
,, J. Tinsley
,, W. Tinsley
L/Cpl. J. W. Tomlinson
Pte. J. W. Tomlinson
,, R. Tomlinson
,, W. Tomlinson
,, J. Tooney
,, A. Topley
,, J. Towers
,, J. Tucker
,, W. J. Tullock
,, F. Turner
,, T. Turner
,, W. Turner
,, C. Tyson
Sgt. J. J. Tyson
Pte. A. Venables
Sgt. E. Vent

Pte. A. E. Vickers
„ R. Vickers
„ W. Vinton
„ F. Wain
„ F. Waitson
„ G. H. Wakefield
„ J. Wakefield
„ W. G. Wakefield
„ D. Walker
„ T. Walker
„ W. Walker
„ W. J. Walker
„ T. Wall
„ R. Wallace
„ G. A. Walmsley
„ R. Walmsley
„ T. Walmsley
„ J. Warburton
„ H. Ward
„ A. Wardle
„ C. E. Warren
„ A. Wassall
„ G. Watkinson
„ W. J. Watson
„ R. Weaver
„ F. Webster
„ P. Webster
Sgt. P. J. Wells
Pte. P. Wesencroft
„ C. Whalley

L/Cpl. A. G. White
Sgt. A. G. White
Pte. E. C. Whiteley
L/Cpl. R. A. Whiteman
Pte. J. F. Whittaker
„ R. Whittle
„ J. Whottan
„ F. Wiggins
„ T. Wignall
„ W. J. Wignall
„ R. Wilcock
„ E. Wild
„ J. Wilding
„ T. Wilkinson
„ T. W. Wilkinson
„ W. Wilkinson
„ C. Williams
„ F. Williams
Cpl. H. Williams
„ H. C. Williams
Pte. J. Williams
„ R. B. Williams
„ S. Williams
„ W. Williams
„ W. Williamson
„ G. B. Wilson
„ H. Wilson
„ J. T. Wilson
„ J. H. Wilson

L/Cpl. H. Wilson
„ J. H. Wilson
Cpl. J. Wilson
Pte. P. Wilson
„ J. Winder
C.S.M. W. H. Winder
L/Cpl. P. H. Wintle
Pte. E. F. Wood
L/Cpl. W. Wood
Pte. E. Woodburn
„ F. G. Woodburn
„ W. Woodburn
„ W. Woodend
„ C. W. Woodhead
„ E. Woodhouse
„ J. Woodruff
„ T. Woods
Cpl. J. Woodward
Pte. S. Woodward
L/Sgt. W. J. Woodward
Pte. W. Woof
„ E. Worth
„ W. Worthington
„ A. J. Wright
L/Sgt. T. Wright
Pte. B. Wyld
„ F. Yarwood
„ R. A. Young

APPENDIX " G."

RANK AND FILE.

MISSING—REPORTED DEAD.

Pte. P. Allen
„ N. Athersmith
„ I. Atkinson

L/Cpl. F. Baines

Cpl. E. W. Barrow

Pte. J. H. Barrow

Cpl. G. Bell

Pte. T. Blezard
„ L. Bowker
„ W. A. Bradley
„ J. Brownlow
„ J. Cameron

L/Cpl. R. Clark

Pte. T. Clark
„ E. Colley
„ J. Cowell
„ H. Cross
„ C. E. Crossley

L/Cp . R. Dobson
,. W. Douglas
Pte. J. Ellis
„ W. Finch
„ F. Futtes
„ J. Halligan
„ E. Hamblett
„ J. Hart
Cpl. N. Hill
Pte. J. Hird
„ J. Hodges
„ S. Hough
„ A. Hulme
„ G. James
„ F. Jenkinson
Cpl. B. A. Lirby
Pte. G. Liddle
„ J. Littleford
„ A. Loftus
„ A. Morris
L/Cpl. T. H. Newby

Pte. J. Owen
„ H. Park
„ R. Postlethwaite
„ J. H. Proctor
L/Cpl. J. Robinson

Pte. J. Simm
„ T. Simpson
„ W. Smith
„ H. J. Snaith
„ G. A. Stenhouse
„ E. Stewart
L/Cpl. W. J. Strode
Pte. W. Swarbrick
Sgt. J. Thistlethwaite
Pte. T. M. Timperley
„ C. H. Turner
„ W. West
„ H. Wilkins
„ T. Williams
„ S. J. Willis
„ A. Wilson

WOUNDED AND PRISONERS.

Pte. R. Allen
Sgt. F. W. Canby
Pte. G. Grosvenor
  ,, J. W. Harrall

Cpl. T. Hird
Pte. T. Leck
  ,, M. Newby
  ,, S. Scotchford

Pte. J. Smith
  ,, T. Smith
  ,, W. Tomlinson
  ,, G. Wilson

WOUNDED AND MISSING.

Pte. A. Bell
  ,, T. Bell
  ,, T. Bowen
L/Cpl. J. Dickie
Pte. R. Garnett
  ,, J. H. Hall
Cpl. T. Hird

Pte. W. Leviston
  ,, J. Logan
  ,, H. Metters
  ,, H. Newby
Sgt. F. N. Postlethwaite
Pte. R. Prisk
  ,, I. T. Rowse

Pte. E. H. Shelton
  ,, H. Sprout
  ,, W. Sykes
Cpl. N. H. Taylor
Pte. F. Williams
  ,, J. J. Wilshaw
  ,, G. H. Wright

MISSING.

Sgt. J. Amos
Pte. J. C. Anson
  ,, H. W. Ashworth
  ,, J. Ashworth
  ,, A. Atkinson
Cpl. T. Atkinson
Pte. J. Atherton
  ,, J. B. Atherton
  ,, A. T. Barron
  ,, J. Barton
  ,, R. Bashall
  ,, A. V. Bell
  ,, A. Bennett
  ,, F. Berry
  ,, S. Berry
  ,, T. B. Blake
  ,, H. Boothman
Sgt. H. Bradley
Pte. J. H. Bradley
  ,, L. Bray
  ,, F. Briggs
  ,, E. H. Brocklebank
  ,, J. T. Brocklebank
  ,, R. Brown
  ,, R. Burrow
  ,, J. Burrows
  ,, J. Capstick
  ,, G. Caton
  ,, P. Chadderton
  ,, W. Clark
Sgt. B. Clarke
Pte. C. Clarkson
  ,, J. Clough
  ,, J. H. Conning
  ,, W. B. Cowper
  ,, A. Crabb
  ,, J. Craig

Pte. A. Crammon
  ,, E. Cross
  ,, A. J. Crossling
  ,, W. Crowther
  ,, J. Cubitt
  ,, S. Date
  ,, T. A. Davies
  ,, T. W. Davies
  ,, B. Dixon
  ,, J. Downham
  ,, H. Doyle
  ,, J. Dunn
  ,, G. H. Durham
  ,, A. Earnshaw
  ,, J. E. Fawcett
  ,, J. Fletcher
  ,, A. Fox
  ,, L. Fox
  ,, C. W. Frearson
  ,, T. Gamble
L/Sgt. G. Grafton
Pte. G. Graveson
       (Prisoner)
  ,, H. Green
  ,, J. B. Greenwood
  ,, M. Grigg
  ,, T. Hacking
Sgt. A. A. Hall
Pte. J. E. Harrison
  ,, W. Harrison
  ,, J. Hartley
  ,, J. H. Hartley
  ,, A. H. Hatton
  ,, W. Hodgson
  ,, R. Horne
  ,, A. E. Hoult
L/Cpl. T. Howcroft

Pte. T. W. Huck
  ,, J. H. Hudson
L/Cpl. P. L. Hunter
Pte. J. W. Ireland
L/Cpl. E. Jackson
Pte. R. James
  ,, T. Jesson
  ,, A. E. Johnson
  ,, C. Johnson
  ,, W. E. Johnson
  ,, E. Jones
  ,, J. L. Jones
  ,, J. Kenny
  ,, T. Leck
  ,, W. Lee
  ,, A. Lord
  ,, J. Lorraine
  ,, W. Lowe
  ,, T. Lowery
  ,, W. J. Lowther
  ,, F. Mallon
L/Cpl. L. Marsden
  ,, F. Marwood
Pte. T. Martin
  ,, J. Mayor
Cpl. J. Miller
Pte. T. Mitchell
  ,, I. Moore
  ,, A. Moorey
  ,, H. B. Mortimer
  ,, A. L. McDonald
  ,, T. McGuire
  ,, T. McKitten
  ,, B. E. Neave
  ,, J. Nelson
  ,, R. Newsham
  ,, W. Nicholson

Pte. W. Nutter
,, J. O'Brien
L/Cpl. A. J. Orders
Pte. J. Orme
,, C. R. Park
,, J. Park
,, W. Parry
,, F. C. Pearce
,, F. Pickthall
,, F. Porter
,, C. Prince
,, R. Ralston
,, J. Remmington
,, E. Rimmer
,, W. Rimmer
,, D. Roberts
,, H. Roberts
,, P. C. Roberts
,, E. G. Robinson

Sgt. H. Robinson
L/Cpl. H. Sanderson
Pte. J. H. Saville
,, J. Schofield
L/Cpl. J. Seabridge
Pte. W. Soddon
,, T. Spencer
,, W. J. Sprout
,, J. Steele
,, W. H. Steenson
,, A. J. Taylor
Sgt. S. Taylor
Pte. J. Theobald
,, J. Threlfall
L/Cpl. E. Topping
Pte. A. Turner
,, T. Turner
,, A. C. Vass
,, A. Walker

Pte. J. Walker
,, F. Walpole
L/Cpl. F. C. Wenham
Pte. R. Whipp
,, T. H. E. Whitehead
,, T. Whitworth
L/Cpl. J. Wilkinson
Pte. T. Wilkinson
,, C. Williams
,, S. Williams
Cpl. C. Wilson
Pte. G. Wilson
,, J. Winder
,, P. Wood
,, E. Woodburn
,, R. Worrall
Sgt. W. Worthington
Pte. F. Wright

PRISONERS OF WAR.

Cpl. T. Atkinson
Pte. J. H. Athersmith
,, J. Atherton
,, H. W. Ashworth
Sgt. T. Amos
L/Cpl. E. D. Askew
Pte. J. Athersmith
L/Cpl. R. Bradshaw
L/Sgt. P. Baines
Pte. E. H. Brocklebank
,, H. Billington
L/Cpl. W. Baxter
Pte. T. Bowen
,, C. E. Barton
,, T. E. Baxter
Sgt. H. Bradley
Pte. R. G. Baxter
,, F. Baines
,, P. Blezard
,, S. Boundy
,, L. Bray
,, H. Bennett
,, J. H. Bradley
,, J. Barton
,, A. F. Barron
,, H. Berry
,, J. Baglin
,, R. Burrow
Sgt. J. Borwick
Pte. R. G. Barrow
Cpl. F. Barker
Pte. W. Brammall
,, W. Barratt
,, J. Clegg
,, E. Clarke
,, J. Clough
,, T. Conroy

Pte. M. Conway
,, G. W. Cole
,, T. Cookson
,, J. Capstick
,, C. Clarkson
,, J. R. Chadwick
,, A. J. Crossing
,, P. Chadderton
,, E. Cross
,, J. H. Conning
,, J. Craven
,, W. Crowther
,, T. W. Davies
,, E. Douglass
,, J. A. Dixon
,, E. Dickinson
,, B. Darcey
,, A. E. Davies
,, T. A. Davis
,, R. Dent
,, A. Dickson
,, F. Evans
,, A. Evans
,, R. Eastwood
,, A. Earnshaw
,, J. J. B. Edgar
Cpl. J. B. Edgar
Pte. R. Elroy
,, L. Fox
,, W. Forbes
Cpl. J. Fairhurst
Pte. G. Graveson
,, W. Gordon
Cpl. W. Galamean
Pte. J. Goldsmith
,, G. Golding
,, W. H. Gaffney

L/Cpl. H. Green
Pte. J. Gilmore
,, F. Gamble
,, A. W. Gould
,, J. B. Greenwood
Sgt. G. Grafton
Pte. W. Harrison
,, H. V. Hudson
,, P. Howarth
L/Cpl. F. Hardman
Pte. J. Howarth
,, S. Holt
,, W. Hodgson
,, B. Horn
,, E. Harper
,, E. Hill
,, R. Helme (Died)
,, T. Hacking
,, P. L. Hunter
,, A. E. Hoult
L/Sgt. A. G. Hall
Pte. H. J. Hall
Cpl. J. Irving
Pte. E. Jones (Died)
,, J. H. Jackson
                (Died)
,, J. L. Jones (Died)
,, R. Jones
,, J. F. Jones
,, J. Jesson
Cpl. R. Johnson
Pte. E. Jackson
,, J. Kelly
,, G. W. Kelton
,, F. Knapp
,, J. Kenny
,, J. Lees

XV

Cpl. J. Lindsay
Pte. R. Lawton
  ,, F. Lindsay
Cpl. H. Lister
Pte. W. Lee
L/Cpl. J. Lowe
Pte. F. W. Lane
  ,, J. Lingard
  ,, W. Lackey
  ,, W. Lowery (Died)
  ,, T. Lowery
  ,, J. Moore
L/Cpl. I. F. Marwood
Pte. W. McNeill
  ,, K. Memory
  ,, J. McDonald
  ,, J. Maxwell
  ,, A. Moorey
Sgt. W. Marshall
Pte. T. McGuire
  ,, I. McKitten
  ,, B. B. Mortimer
  ,, T. Mayor
  ,, J. Nicholson
  ,, F. J. Nicholls
  ,, B. E. Neave
  ,, W. Nicholson
  ,, R. Orrell
  ,, E. O'Neill
  ,, G. E. Park

Pte. W. A. Peach
  ,, C. Prince
  ,, J. G. Pinkney
  ,, J. Park
  ,, W. A. Pepper
  ,, W. Parry
  ,, H. Rigg
Sgt. H. Robinson
Pte. E. W. Rimmer
  ,, R. H. Reay
  ,, R. Ralston
  ,, W. Rimmer
  ,, E. H. Roberts
  ,, H. Skirrow
  ,, F. Stephenson
L/Cpl. W. Shirt
Sgt. F. Sherley
L/Cpl. W. H. Steel
  ,, H. Sanderson
Pte. R. Simpson
  ,, W. Seddon
L/Cpl. J. Steel
  ,, A. Seabridge
Pte. W. Sharpe
  ,, W. Troughton
Cpl. F. H. Turner
Pte. W. Shipperbottom
             (Died)
  ,, A. J. Taylor
  ,, W. H. Turner

Pte. A. Turner
L/Cpl. C. E. Taylor
Pte. R. Taylor
  ,, E. F. Topping
  ,, J. Theobald
L/Sgt. W. Travis
Pte. J. Unsworth
  ,, A. C. Vass
L/Cpl. A. Whittle
Pte. J. Waltho
  ,, T. Williams
  ,, J. J. Woodruff
  ,, J. Worsley
  ,, T. H. E. Whitehead
  ,, E. S. Wood (Died)
  ,, F. Ward
  ,, J. Winder
  ,, W. L. Williams
  ,, J. Woodruffe
Sgt. C. Williams
Pte. C. W. Wells
L/Cpl. J. Wilkinson
Pte. R. Worrall
  ,, A. Walker
  ,, T. Whitworth
Sgt. W. Worthington
Pte. G. R. C. Weedon

APPENDIX " H."

RANK AND FILE—AWARDS.

VICTORIA CROSS.

L/Sgt. T. F. Mayson   Cpl. J. Hewitson

MILITARY CROSS.

C.S.M. R. A. Williams   Sgt. W. Bell

DISTINGUISHED CONDUCT MEDAL.

Sgt. J. S. Owen
Cpl. A. E. Graves
Sgt. R. Adamson
Sgt. A. J. Burton
L/Sgt. G. Johnston

Cpl. H. Martin
L/Cpl. J. Carrick
Sgt. J. M. Cross
  ,, J. R. Pearson
  ,, G. Huddleston

Sgt. W. H. Farish
Pte. C. S. Milton
C.S.M. D. Graham
  ,, J. B. Cook
Sgt. H. Dickinson, M.M.

MILITARY MEDAL.

Pte. A. E. Ashburn
Cpl. T. Balderston
Pte. T. Binns
Sgt. J. Birkett
Pte. R. Bradley
,, J. Bussingham
Cpl. R. Carruthers
,, J. Carton
Sgt. T. J. Chapple
L/Cpl. T. Chester
Pte. J. Cooley
L/Cpl. C. F. Cooper
Pte. T. Cross (and Bar)
Cpl. C. W. Crichton
L/Cpl. W. Danson
L/Sgt. H. Dickinson,
　　　　　D.C.M.
Sgt. H. Fearnley
Pte. H. Green
,, H. Helme

L/Cpl. G. Hewartson
L/Cpl. R. F. Hinde
C.Q.M.S. W. G. Hinds
C.S.M. G. Holme
Sgt. A. C. Holmes
,, A. H. Jackson
Cpl. F. Jackson
Sgt. R. N. Jackson
,, R. Lockey
Pte. L. Marsden
,, G. Mackereth
Sgt. T. H. Middleton
　　　　　(and Bar)
,, A. Morris
,, H. Myers
Pte. J. McAlarney
L/Cpl. W. McGill
Pte. W. Nicholson
Sgt. H. Parnell ....

Sgt. H. W. Perceval
Pte. G. Poskitt
Sgt. T. G. Rathbone
Pte. E. Redpath
,, E. G. Robinson
Sgt. T. Robinson
Cpl. F. A. Sherley
L/Sgt. H. Smith
Pte. P. Stalker
,, H. Stott
,, R. Taylor
,, J. W. Thomas
L/Cpl. H. Q. Towers
Cpl. P. J. Vernoun
Pte. G. Wakefield
,, G. H. Watson
Sgt. W. T. Whiteside
Pte. J. Wild
L/Sgt. T. Wright

MENTIONED IN DESPATCHES.

C.S.M. W. Bell
Sgt. J. Coward
,, W. Hayhurst

Sgt. R. N. Jackson
A/R.S.M. J. Way
L/Cpl. P. Baines

L/Cpl. T. Jackson
Pte. J. A. Kitchen

BRONZE MEDAL FOR MILITARY VALOUR.

C.S.M. R. Walker

BELGIAN CROIX-DE-GUERRE.

Sgt. G. B. Collins

MERITORIOUS SERVICE MEDAL.

R.Q.M.S. W. Clark   Sgt. S. Hinds   Sgt. W. Rickwood

APPENDIX " I."

Extract from the Supplement dated 28th June, 1918, to the " London Gazette " dated 25th June, 1918.

WAR OFFICE, 28TH JUNE, 1918.

His Majesty The King has been graciously pleased to approve of the award of the Victoria Cross to the undermentioned Officers, Non-Commissioned Officers and Men :—

*   *   *   *   *

2nd Lieut. JOSEPH HENRY COLLIN, late Royal Lancaster Regiment.

For most conspicuous bravery, devotion to duty and self-sacrifice in action.

After offering a long and gallant resistance against heavy odds in the Keep held by his platoon, this officer, with only five of his men remaining, slowly withdrew in the face of superior numbers, contesting every inch of the ground. The enemy were pressing him hard with bombs and machine-gun fire from close range. Single-handed 2nd Lieutenant Collin attacked the machine gun and team. After firing his revolver into the enemy, he seized a Mills grenade and threw it into the hostile team, putting the gun out of action, killing four of the team and wounding two others. Observing a second hostile machine gun firing, he took a Lewis gun, and selecting a high point of vantage on the parapet whence he could engage the gun, he, unaided, kept the enemy at bay until he fell mortally wounded.

The heroic self-sacrifice of 2nd Lieutenant Collin was a magnificent example to all.

APPENDIX " J."

Extract from the Supplement dated 14th September, 1917, to the " London Gazette " dated 14th September, 1917.

WAR OFFICE, 14TH SEPTEMBER, 1917.

His Majesty The King has been graciously pleased to approve of the award of the Victoria Cross to the undermentioned Officers, Non-Commissioned Officers, and Men :—

*   *   *   *   *

No. 200717, Corpl. (L/Sgt.) TOM FLETCHER MAYSON, Royal Lancaster Regiment (Silecroft, Cumberland).

For most conspicuous bravery and devotion to duty when with the leading wave of the attack his platoon was held up by machine gun fire from a flank.

Without waiting for orders, L/Sgt. Mayson at once made for the gun, which he put out of action with bombs, wounding four of the team. The remaining three of the team fled, pursued by L/Sgt. Mayson to a dugout into which he followed them, and disposed of them with his bayonet.

Later, when clearing up a strong point, this non-commissioned officer again tackled a machine gun single-handed, killing six of the team.

Finally, during an enemy counter-attack, he took charge of an isolated post, and successfully held it till ordered to withdraw as his ammunition was exhausted.

He displayed throughout the most remarkable valour and initiative.

APPENDIX " K."

Extract from the Supplement dated 28th June, 1918, to the " London Gazette " dated 25th June, 1918.

THE WAR OFFICE, 28TH JUNE, 1918.

His Majesty The King has been graciously pleased to approve of the award of the Victoria Cross to the undermentioned Officers, Non-Commissioned Officers, and Men :—

*   *   *   *   *

No. 15883, Lance-Corporal JAMES HEWITSON, Royal Lancaster Regiment (Coniston).

For most conspicuous bravery, initiative and daring in action.

In a daylight attack on a series of crater posts, L/Cpl. Hewitson led his party to their objective with dash and vigour, clearing the enemy from both trench and dug-outs, killing in one dug-out six of the enemy who would not surrender. After capturing the final objective, he observed a hostile machine-gun team coming into action against his men. Working his way round the edge of the crater he attacked the team, killing four and capturing one. Shortly afterwards he engaged a hostile bombing party, which was attacking a Lewis-gun post. He routed the party, killing six of them.

The extraordinary feats of daring performed by this gallant N.C.O. crushed the hostile opposition at this point.

INDEX.

INDEX.—*Continued*.

CROWTHER & GOODMAN,
PRINTERS,
124, FENCHURCH STREET, LONDON, E.C. 3.